MASHUP

Mary LaForge

Gallery

ISBN 13: 978-81-8253-891-7

First Edition: 2022
Rs. 600/- $27

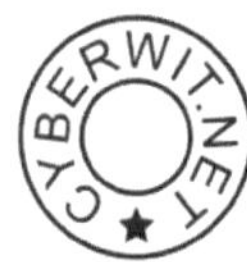

Cyberwit.net
HIG 45 Kaushambi Kunj, Kalindipuram
Allahabad - 211011 (U.P.) India
http://www.cyberwit.net
Tel: +(91) 9415091004 +(91) (532) 2552257
E-mail: info@cyberwit.net

Printed at Repro India Limited.

The Mary LaForge Gallery is proud to present the work of emerging artist Alice Shapiro in its first year of exhibition programming. Shapiro's miniature digital collage visually explores the idea of heritage with a new perspective both in her narrative art and with personal stories.

Mary LaForge Gallery exhibits collage artworks as sister exhibitions to global art fairs and art and business conferences from its online gallery.

Introduction

Cultural identity and genetic ancestry do not always line up. There is no genetics of culture." -- The Genetics of Culture (Hint: It doesn't exist) by Chelsea Weidman, geneticsdigest.com

The Premise.

The article goes on to say even though the vast majority of human DNA is the same, you cannot tell where your ancestors came from because DNA testing only considers current living populations. Culture can be your grandmother's traditional biscuit recipe or stories about emigrating to America. So, without a place of origin and without folklore about cultural practices in "the old country," third-generation Americans such as me have literally no heritage or culture to identify us as a separate and unique group of peoples. Especially in large cities, we become a mashup of many cultures.

By visually exploring the concept of the absence of ancestral heritage I attempt to alleviate the "not belonging" anxiety of myself and others through the medium of digital art miniatures. Art, whether creating it or viewing it intentionally, is a natural though often inexplicable medium capable of providing emotional serenity and focus. During my search to find a historically placed individual me, I unwittingly uncovered a simple yet profound personal purpose to serve others: Share Beauty. This book attempts to convey, in imagery and stories, an individual beauty and essence that exists within the cultures I've been exposed to, as much as an artist can hope to express within a body of work. -- Alice Shapiro

Discovering An Authentic Artistic Voice.

My style of artmaking was primarily influenced around 9 years of age by seeing Picasso's Three Musicians and one of Dali's desert melting clock paintings side-by-side in a magazine ad. Later influences I adopted include Paul Klee, Joseph Cornell, Kurt Schwitters, and Marcel Duchamp. The accumulated genre that arose from my art-centered environment as a Narrative Mashup Style is a combination of those influences, namely Cubism, Surrealism, Bauhaus, Assemblage, Collage, and Dada.

Prior to 2017 my artwork consisted of pastel, oil and acrylic portraiture and modernist paintings with a sporadic exploration into clay sculpture especially during my gallerist days in the miniature studio gallery I ran. A tentative exploration then into digitally producing art online blossomed exponentially after discovering Canva. I found the marketing design platform to be elastic enough to generate depth and emotion in my digital paintings regardless of the limited program of marketing-purposed assets, and perhaps because of it.

Graduating from SUNY Farmingdale with an A.A.S. Degree in Advertising Art and Design I came full circle to begin a career of balancing the seemingly opposite worlds of Studio Art and Business Design. There again the search for a "voice," a "belonging to" identity took many decades to reconcile and fuse into a recognizable style of my own. Perhaps merging of the two occupations is one reason I feel comfortable and joyful in the struggle to create an authentic work. It affords me a sense of truth as to who I am outside the arbitrary labels of heritage and culture.

CHAPTER one

OTHER CULTURES.

This chapter covers my imaginary and actual travels through Russia and Eastern Europe, Africa, India, American Northeast, American Southeast, France, and China.

During the early exploration into my past I realized the futility of tracing details and decided instead to focus on the beauty inherent in objects and photographs taken by others depicting different Indigenous cultures that weren't mine in actuality or spirit. I could then combine them with elements from my American sphere, and together perhaps I believed I might discover who I am, at least culturally.

Russia and Eastern Europe.

I'm a third generation American. Grandparents emigrated from somewhere in Russia, maybe Kiev, and Eastern Europe. They never told stories of their homelands. We only heard English words spoken except for a few snippets when grown-ups were exclusively privy to the content. We didn't attend religious institutions and only had two very brief semi-traditional ceremonies each year until I was 12, and then nothing. Our neighborhood was filled with second generation Europeans and their offspring who were also waning away from their traditional roots. What remained was a hodgepodge of cultures outwardly different than mine and yet I assimilated into them as a feelingness. These were my people. We were Americans. Hard-working, joyful, and helpfully bonded together.

The exception to this scenario was my mother's mother. While she didn't speak about her past adult life, Grandma did share her traumatic childhood experience of being placed in an orphanage. Evidently this was an option for a parent struggling financially. Grandma's father had passed away and left her mother with three small children to raise alone. Grandma was sent away until her mother remarried and was able to rejoin the family. Grandma's story gets even more interesting when she recounts a bullying incident at the orphanage. I don't remember exactly how it went down but Grandma won the respect of the offenders with something about Grandma wielding a knife stolen from the dinner table. Brava Grandma! We were fortunate to have Grandma with us for her 96 years. She lived in her own apartment until the last year and was admitted to a relatively decent "home" facility. Pretty sad though that Grandma had to relive an institutional situation.

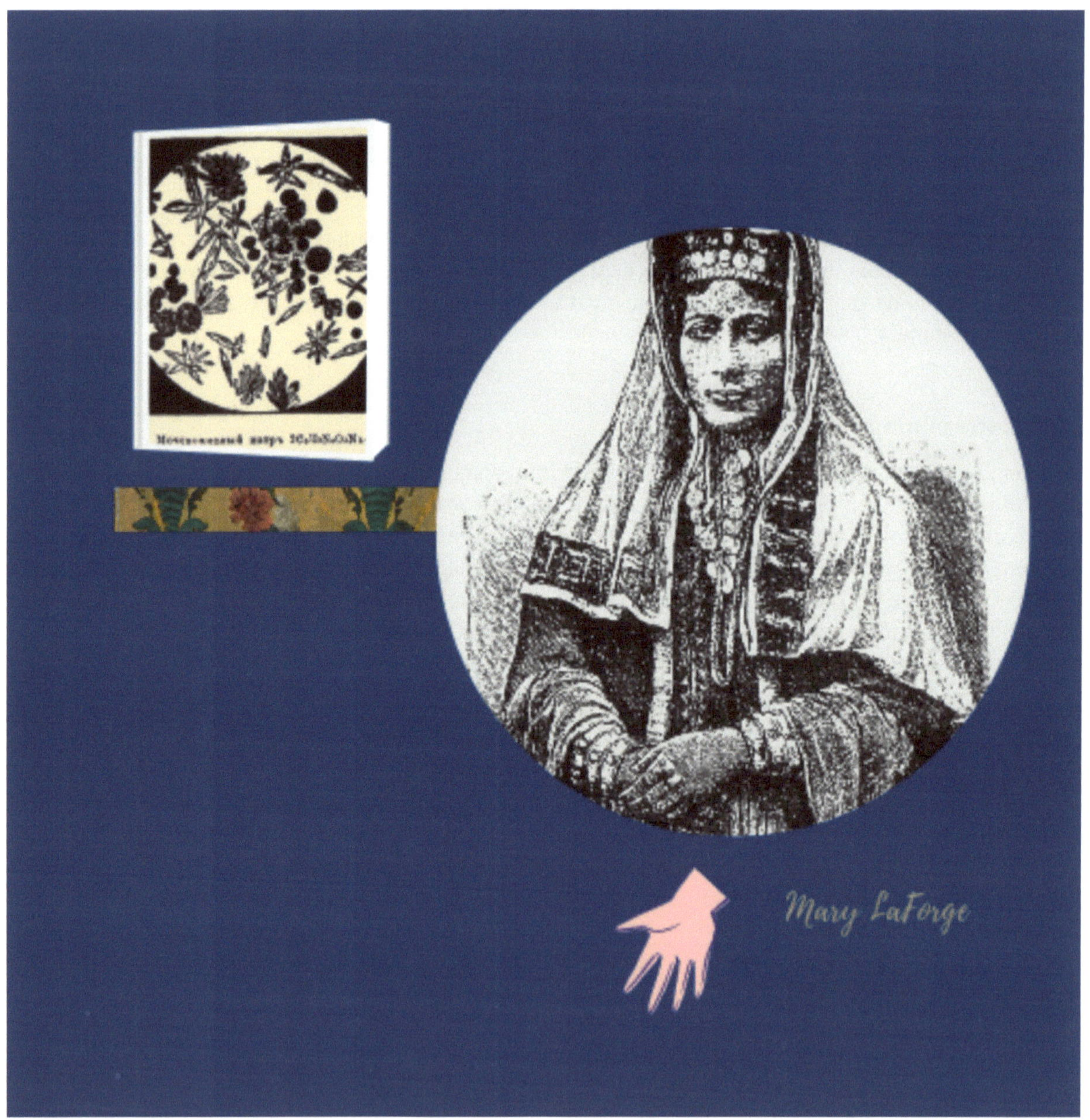

Fabric of Royalty

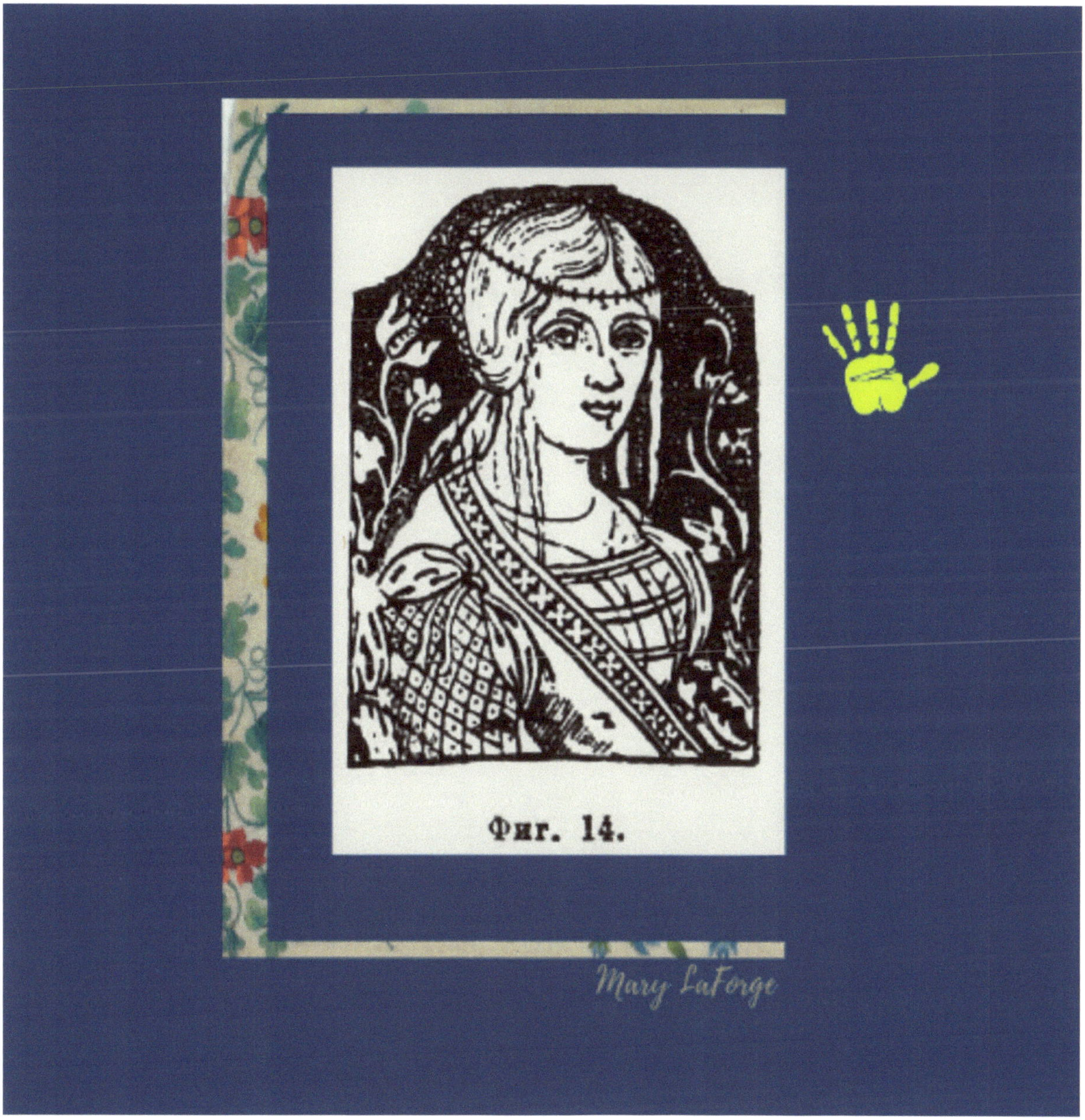

Woman In Woodcut

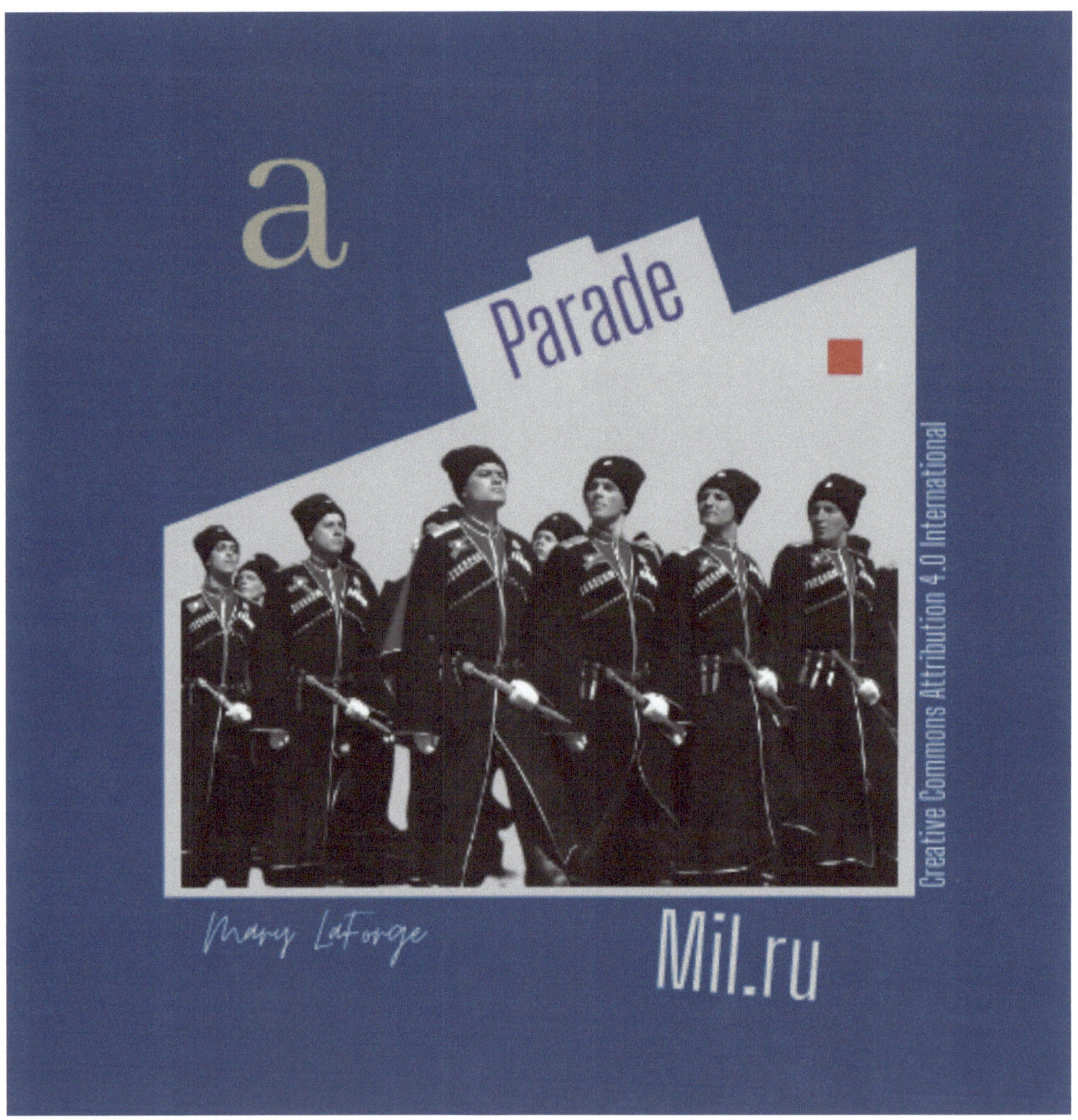

Parade Red Square

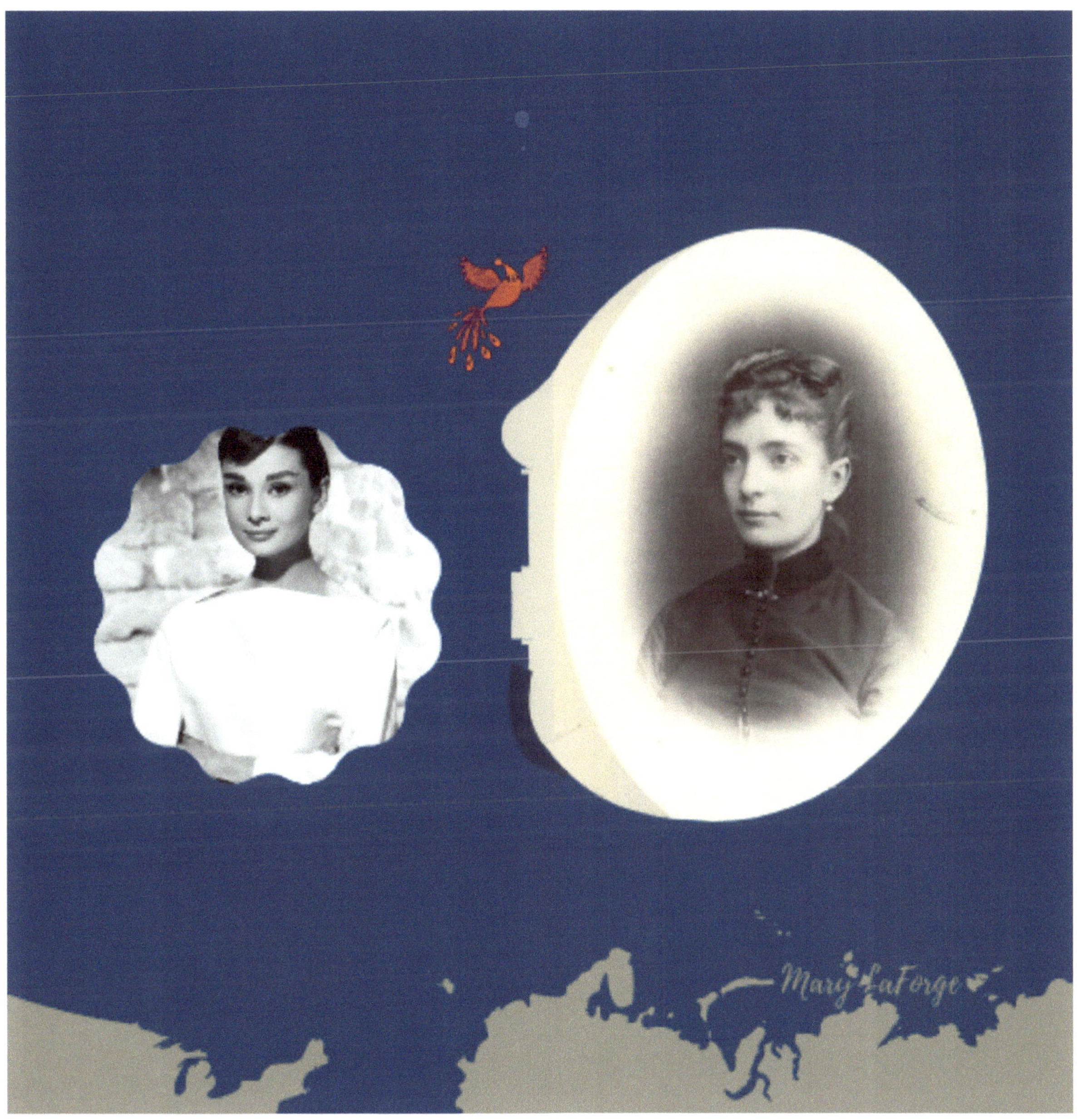

Anonymously Crossing Barriers

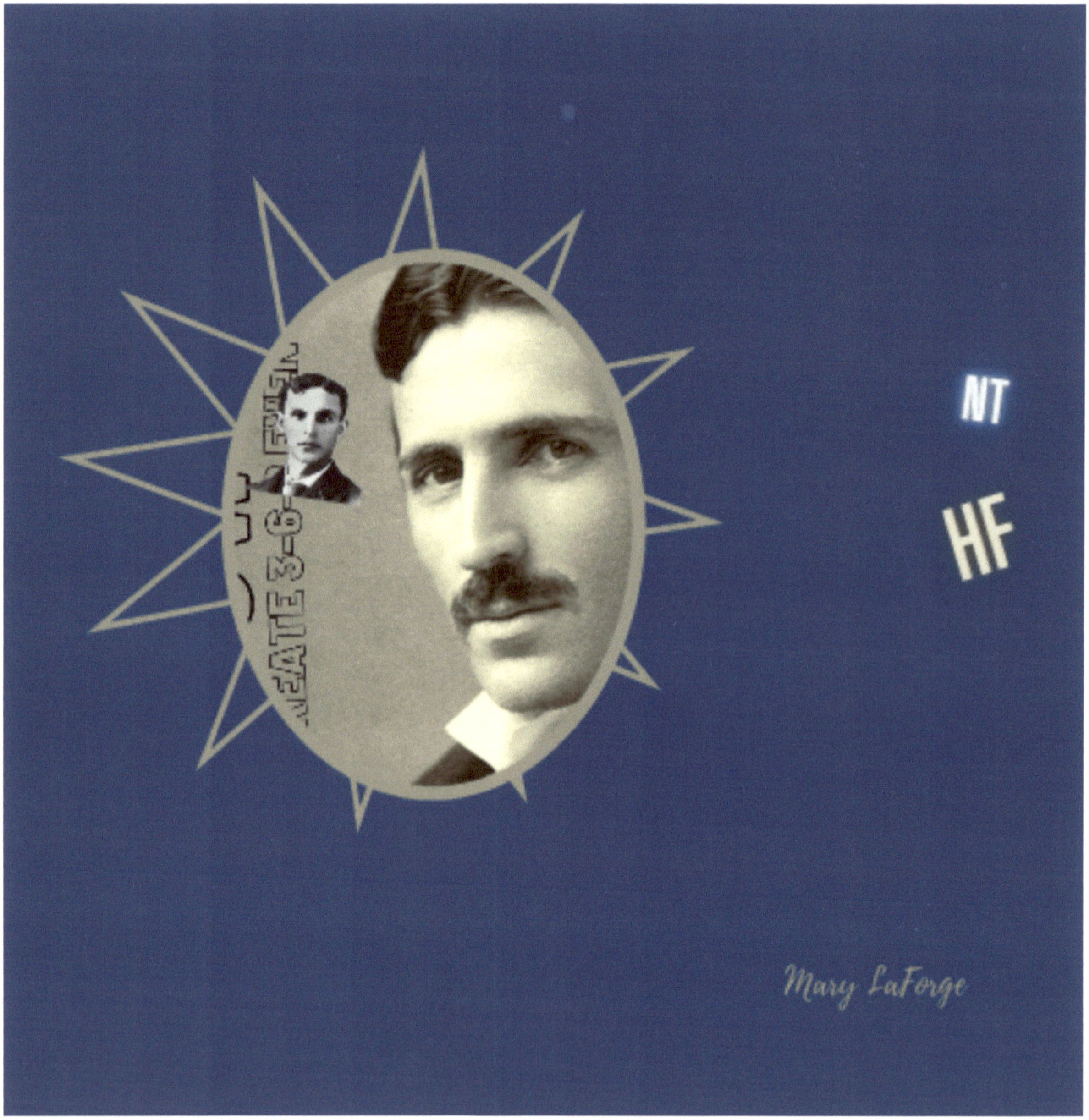

The Tesla-Ford Paradigm

Africa.

On my way to learning more about who I am culturally I saw there are various ways to approach self discovery. One cinematographer chronicled her one-year escape from society in beautiful nature scenes and an emotionally spoken narrative about her personal pain. Many related to her emotional situation. Another approach is to be factual like anthropological explorations. There's also the Confessional style of total psychological venting such as the Poet Sylvia Plath, who unfortunately committed suicide. I could make lists – my 5 most common traits. Instead, this art book fits better as a straightforward presentation with a focus on three elements - heading, narrative, images.

When I worked at the Metropolitan Museum of Art I felt I was literally experiencing an aspect of heaven. Daily lunch hours were spent in the galleries; my favorite day was Monday when the Museum was closed to the public. One of the artifacts that resonated with me was The Dogon Couple housed in the African Art Gallery. Peripherally perhaps I absorbed a bit of the Dogon culture by observing the work of art many, many times, and from my imagination possibly came to know the unknown artist's process of creating. In this way we were fused as creative family, not of the Earth, yet in the Air. I felt how we are all connected culturally through art.

Some art takes a minimum amount of time to create when all the elements line up. Art such as the Bobo image however was created with layers upon layers of digital assets over the course of 3 days and approximately 49 hours.

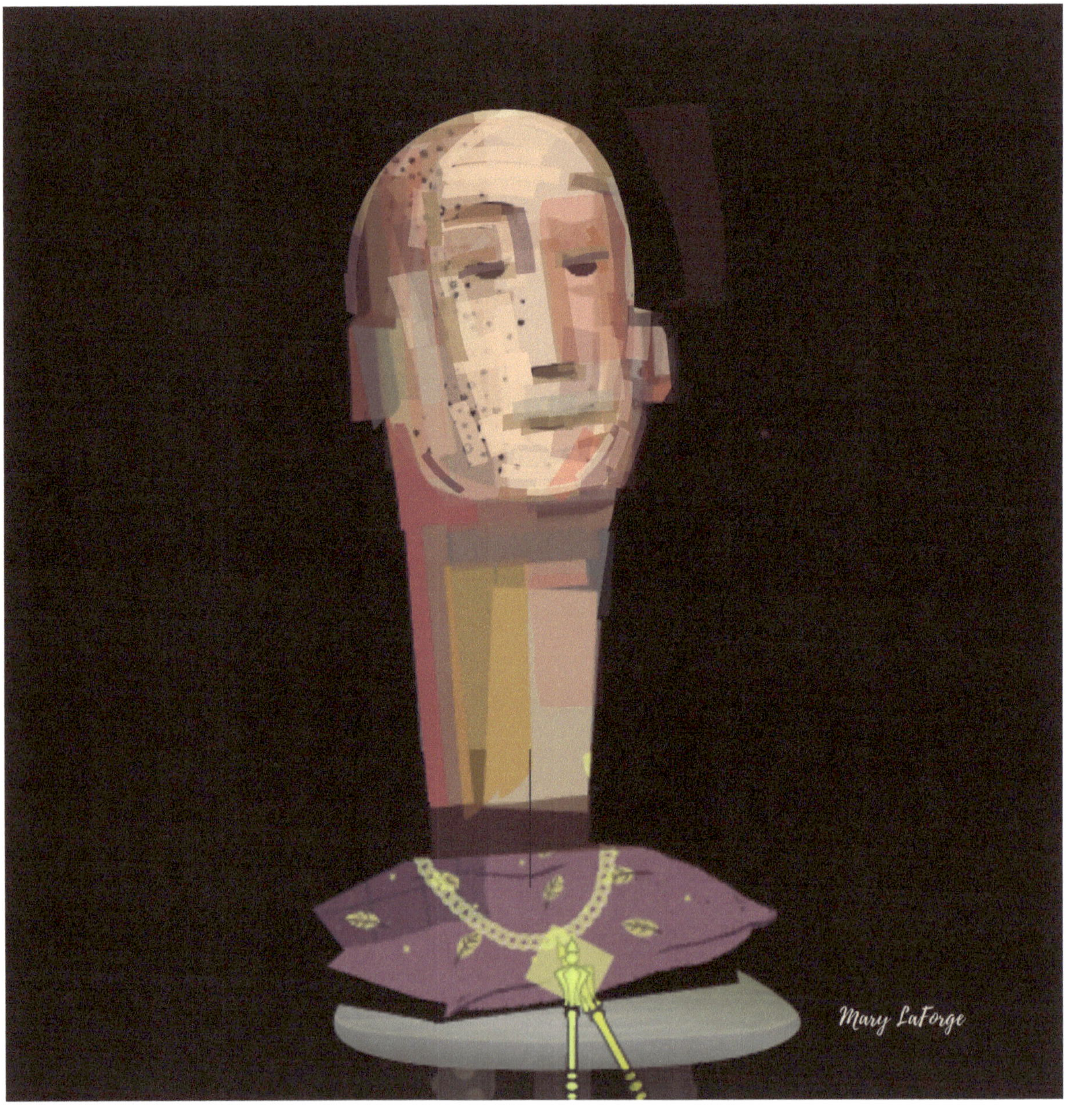

Bobo

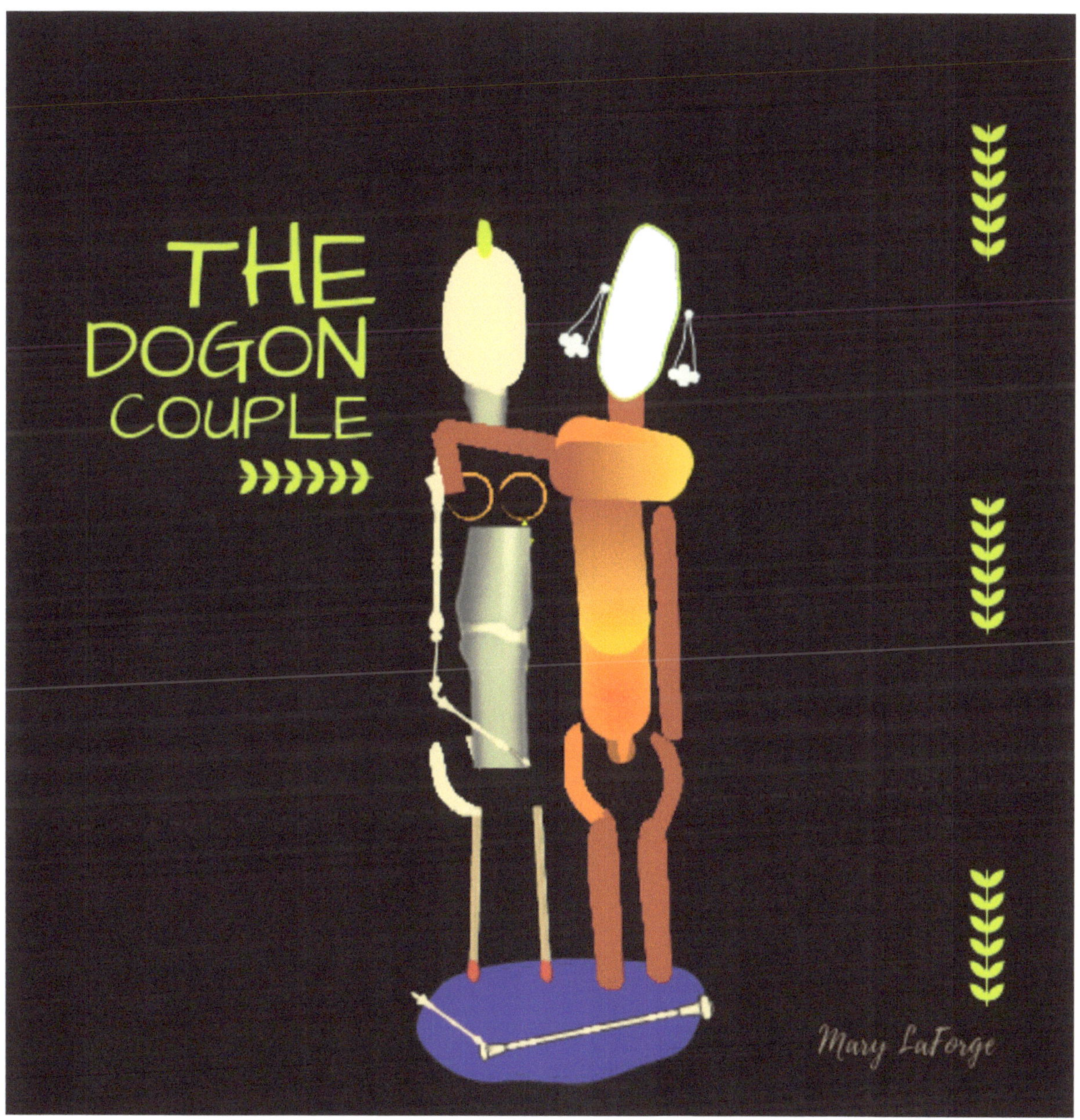

Seated Dogon Couple

India.

I traveled to India, twice. Each visit lasted around a month. Leaving the overcast and stressful New York City environment of bustling people mostly silently scurrying to jobs with blank faces, I had a bit of culture shock entering the wide open dusty landscape of Indian sunshine blazing in the vast cerulean sky and spotted with the richest of colors and patterns worn by beautiful women. I pondered the happiness of my taxi driver as he coughed the dusty distance while proudly pointing out important sites along our path. He absolutely loved his country!

I craft these miniature digital collages as a physical activity I enjoy doing and as a visual feast for others, knowing in the end these are objects that have a limited existence. No matter how long they may last into future generations, like all else, when my life spirit leaves my physical body, I cannot take them with me.

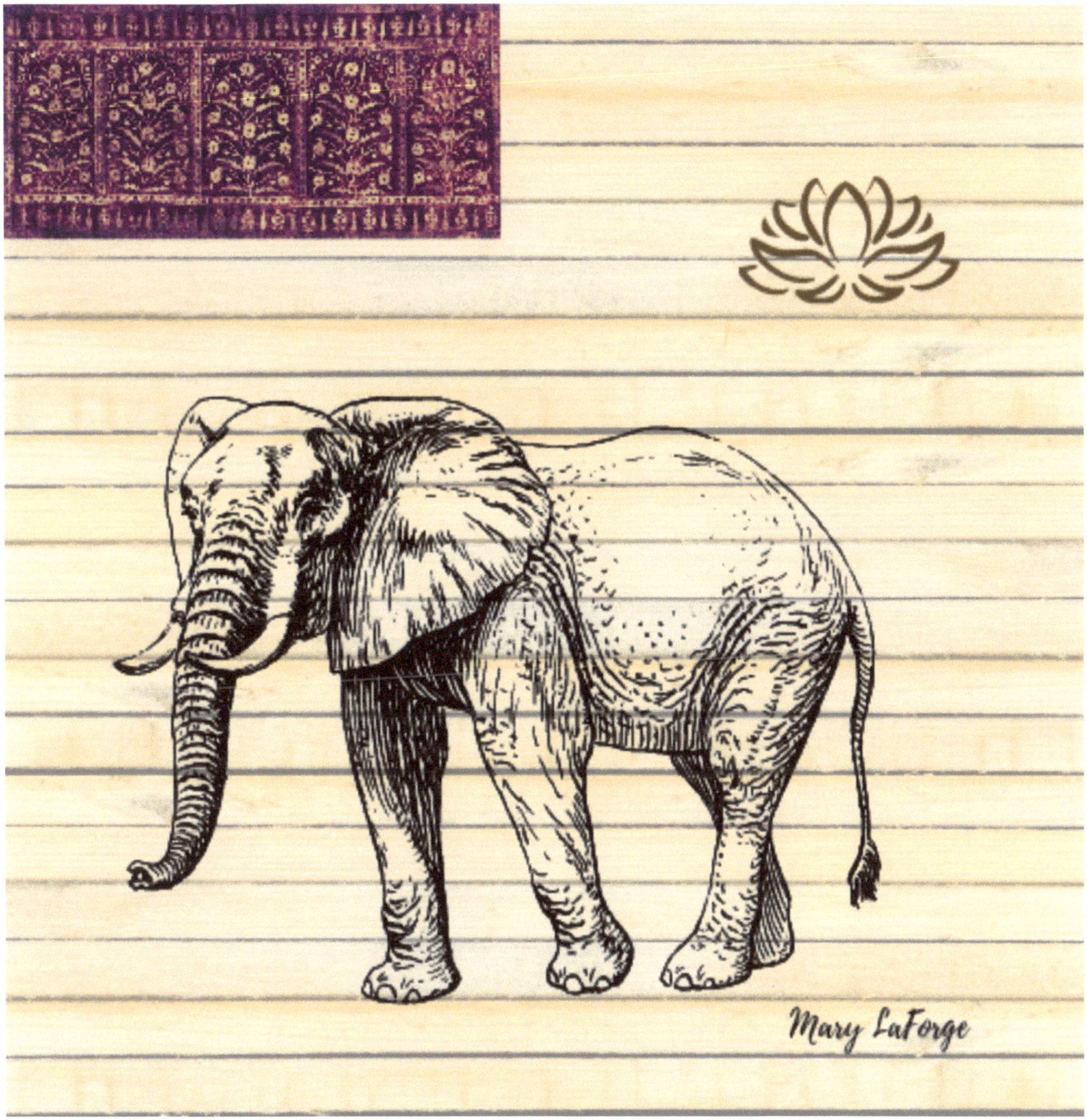

Elephant

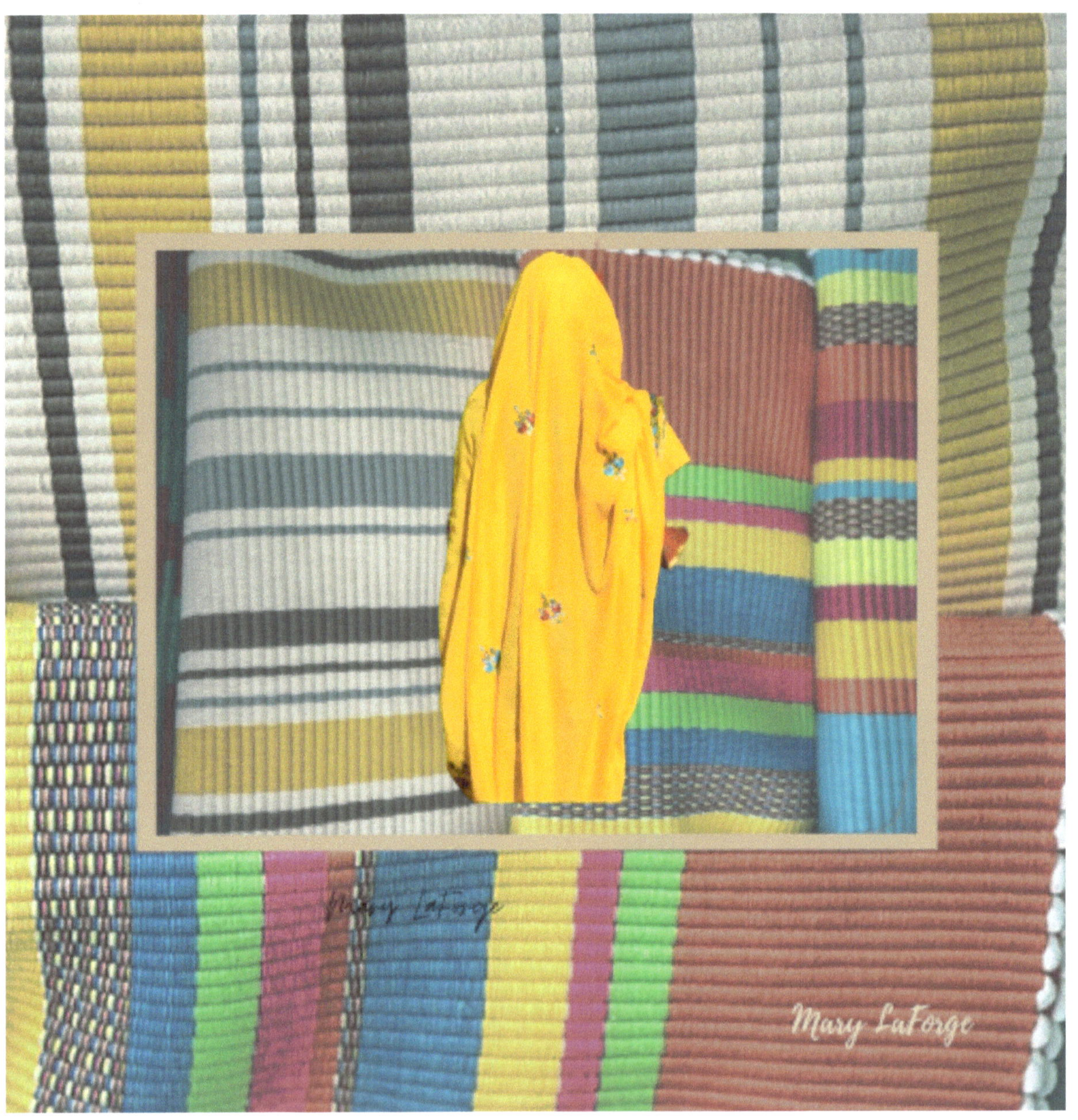

Sari

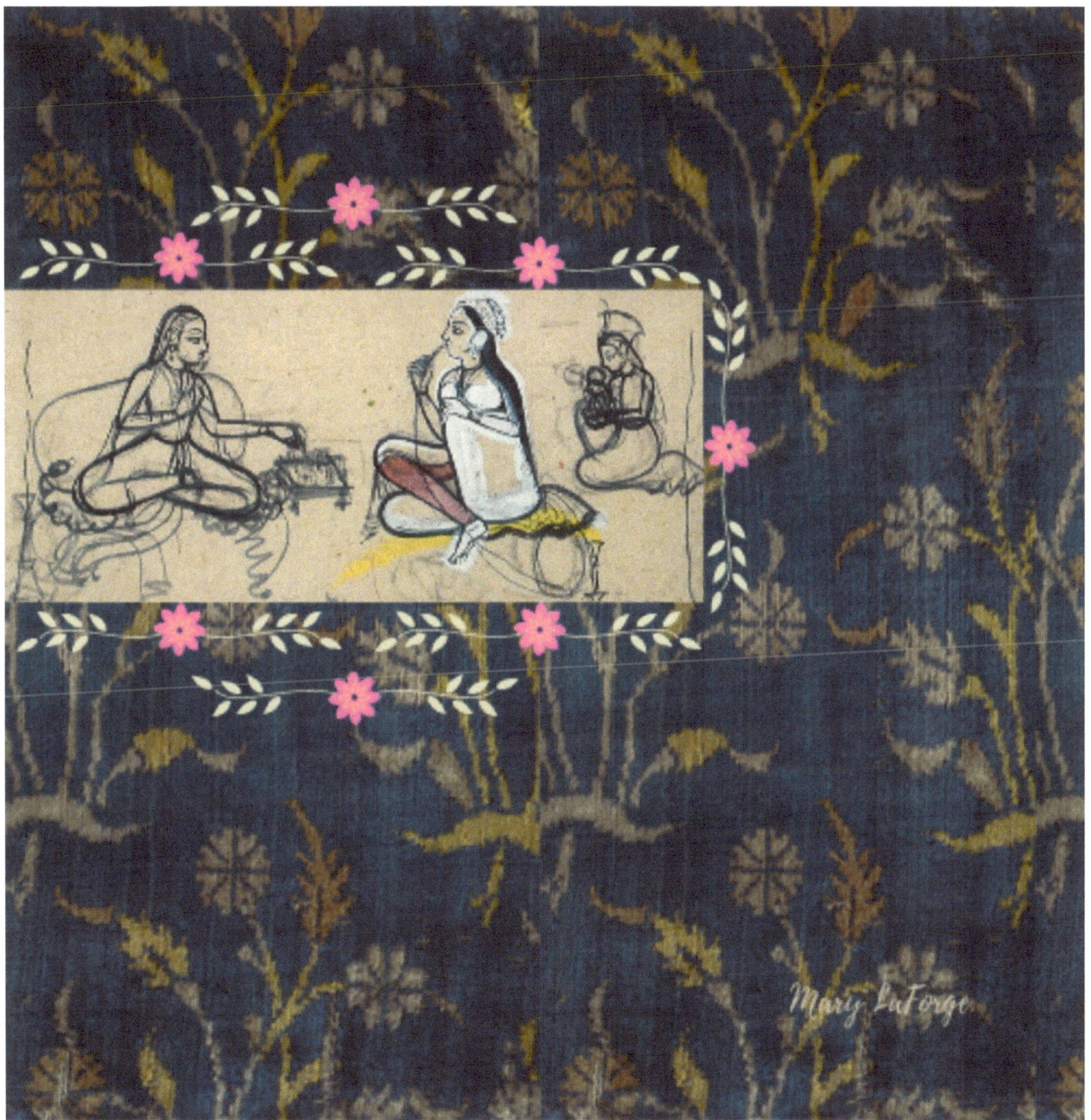

Chess Players Textiles

American Northeast.

The story goes that Grandmother had the task of taking me downtown in my carriage to watch the parade. Most likely it was Memorial Day or Fourth of July. While she was distracted by the pomp and circumstance I had managed to climb out and was hanging down the side of the carriage, safely dangling by the harness around my body, evidently enjoying the festivities immensely. Grandmother, not surprisingly, was quite panicked when she noticed I was gone.

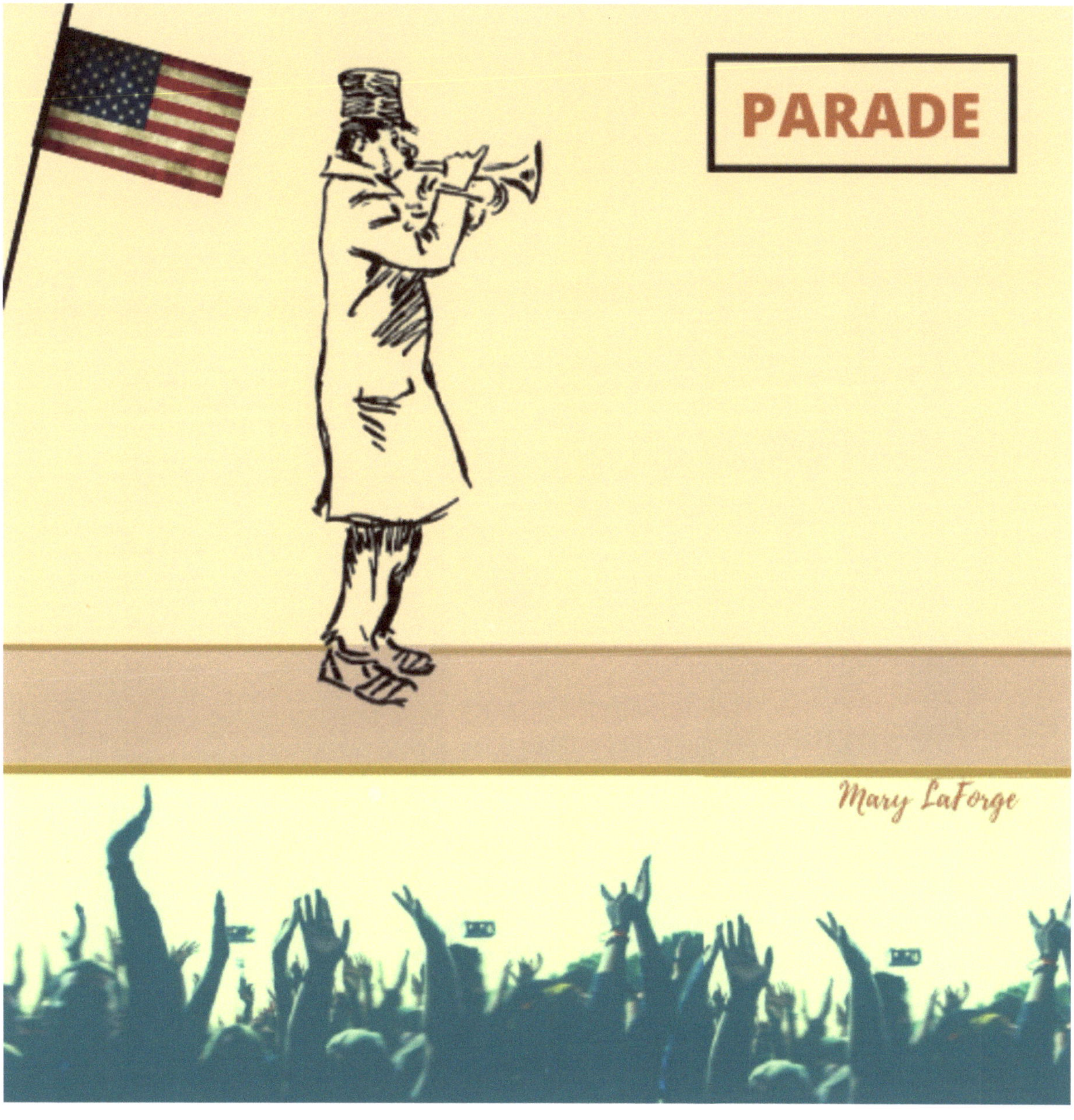

Downtown Parade

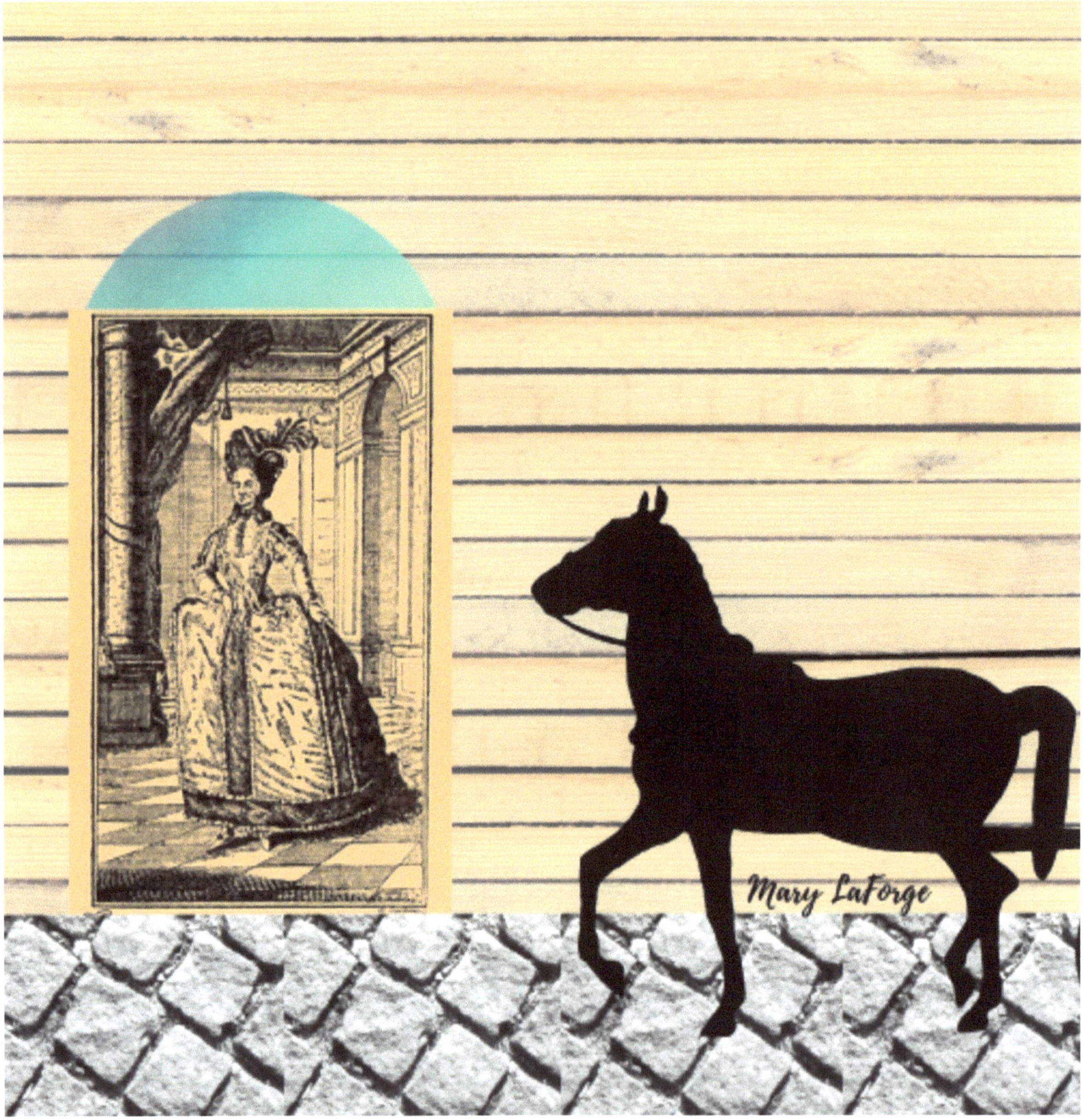

Door Etiquette

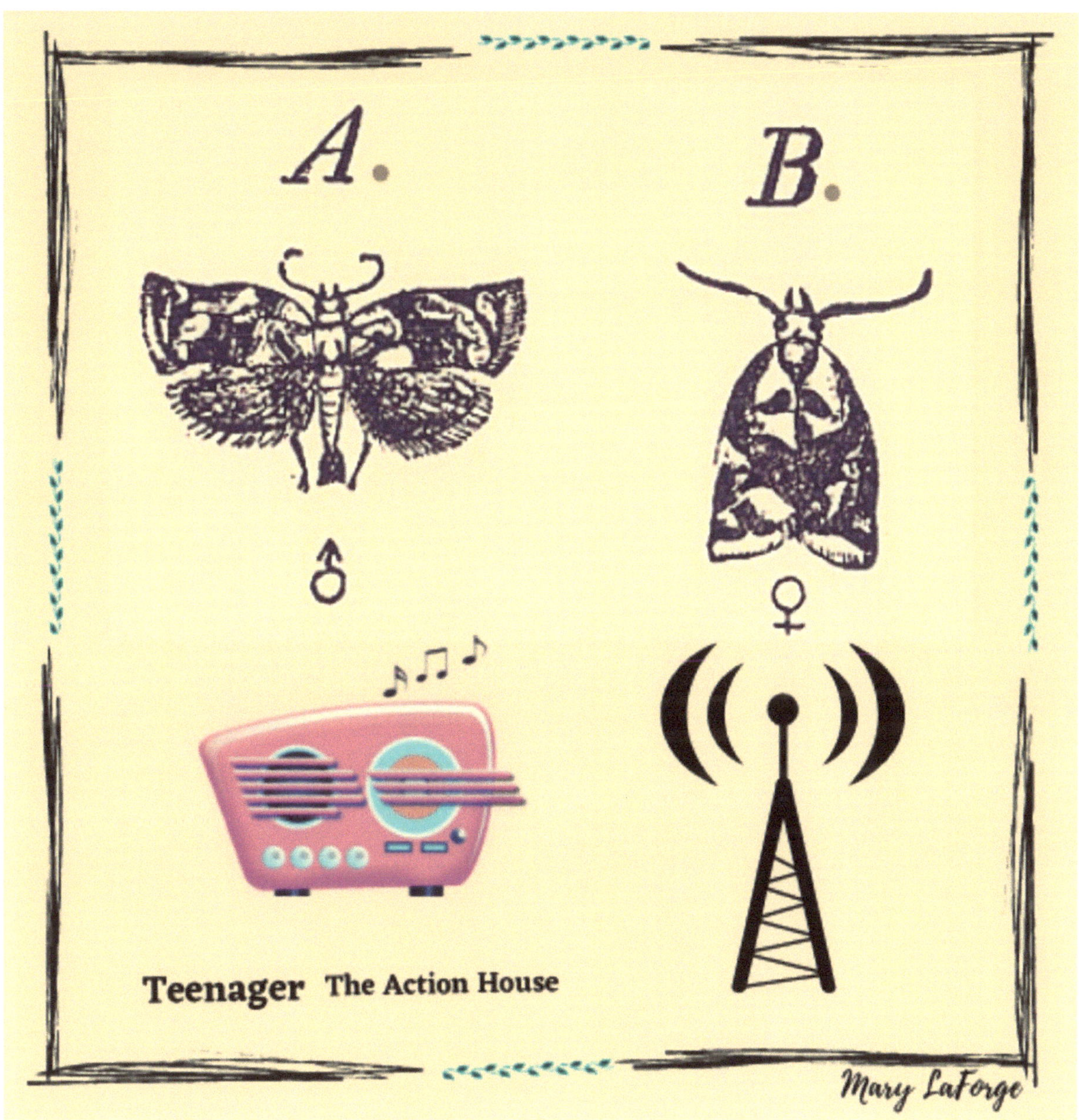

Action House Disco

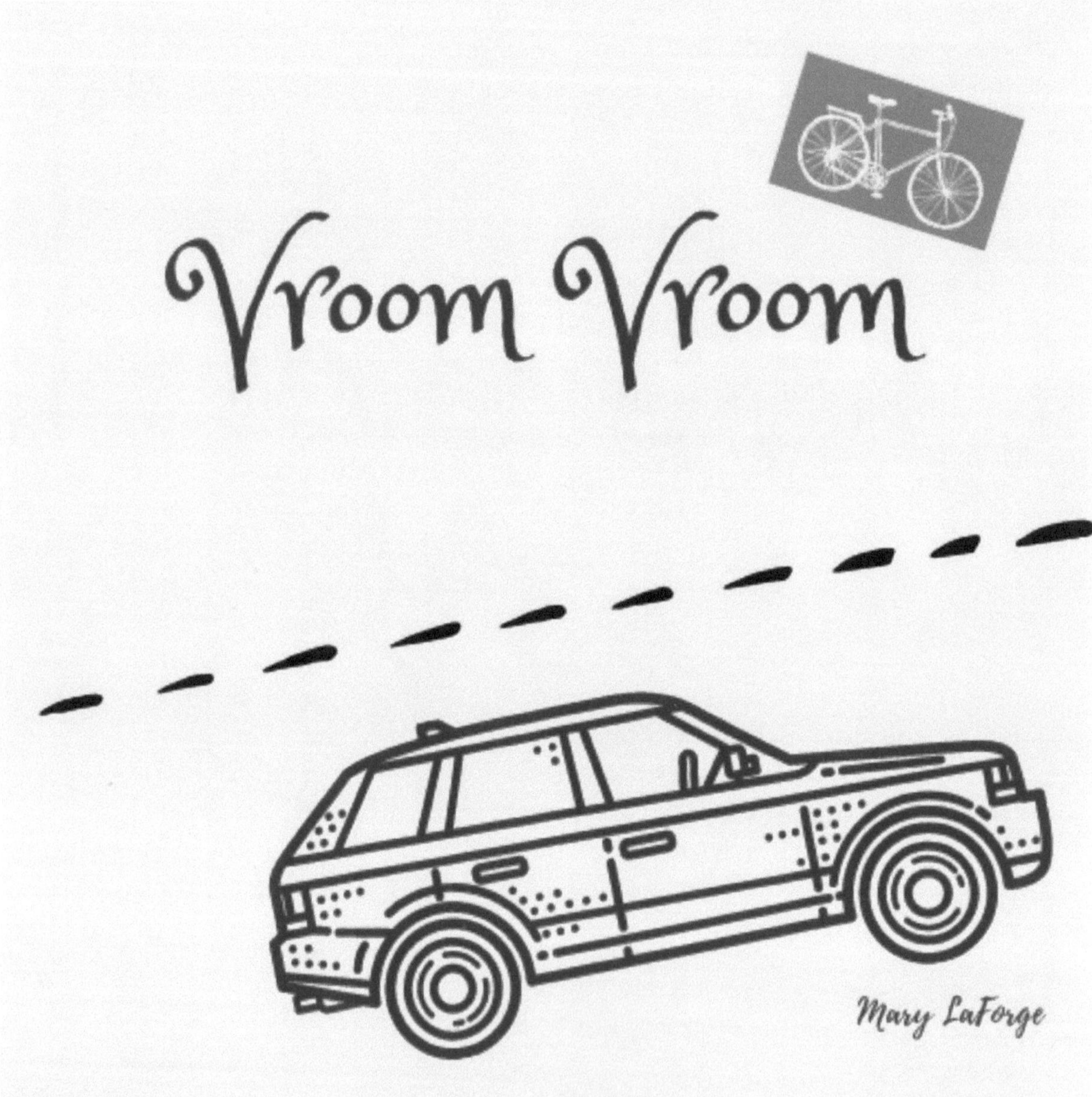

Station Wagon Drive-In

American Southeast.

I've lived in the South for 17 years. I've become more polite and wish I could curb sarcasm quicker. Nature is healing.

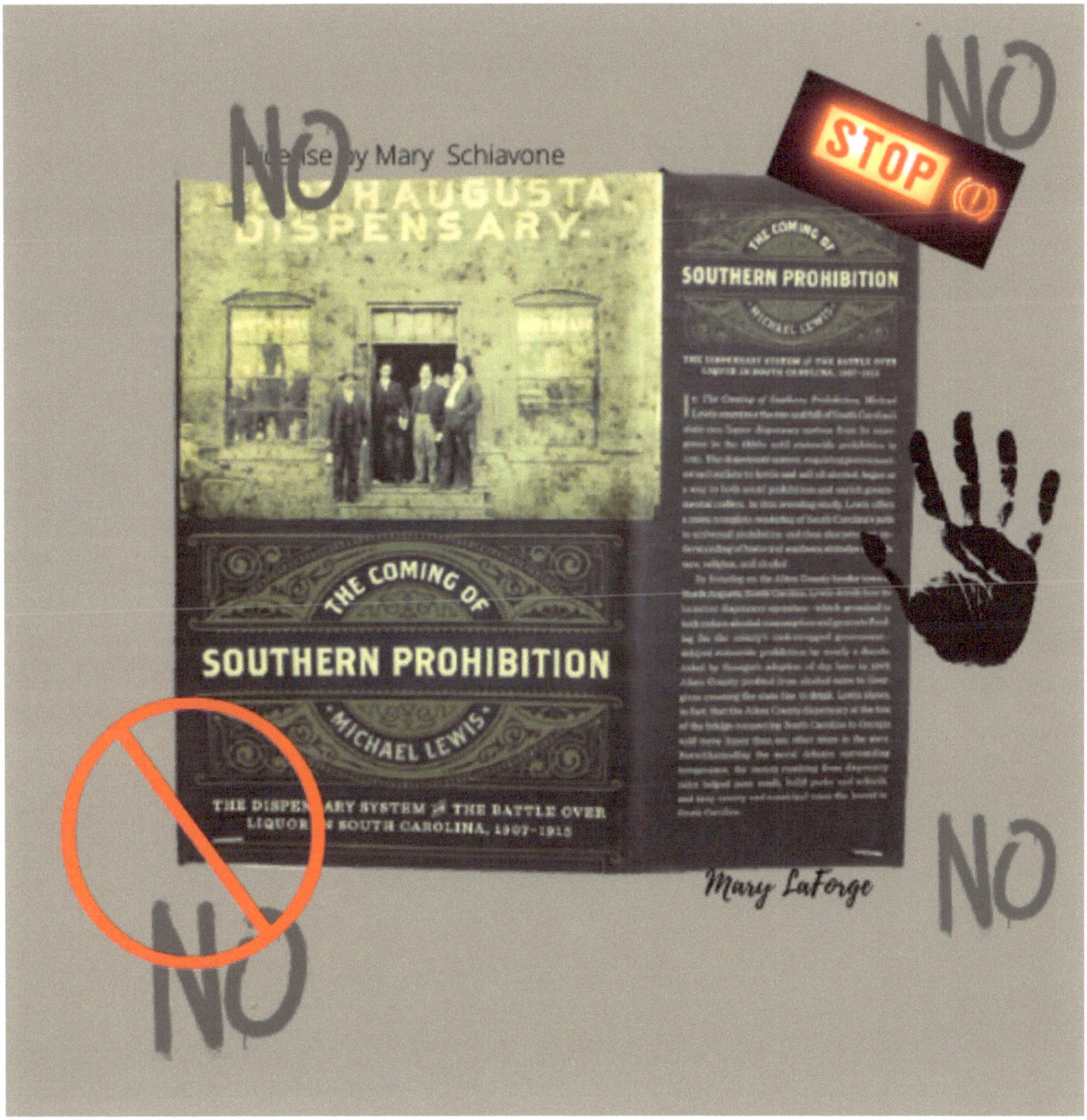

Prohibition

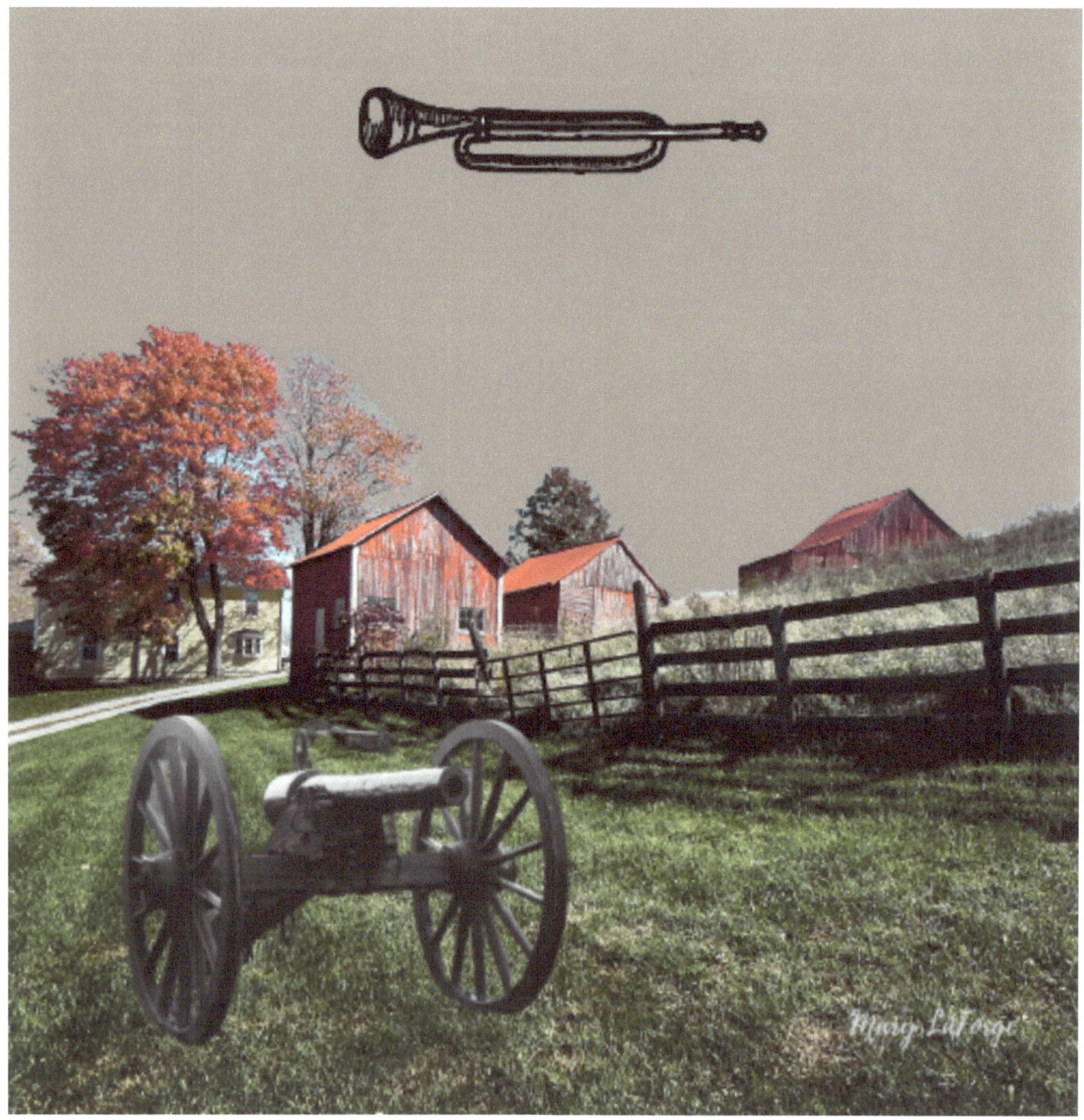

Lawn Decor

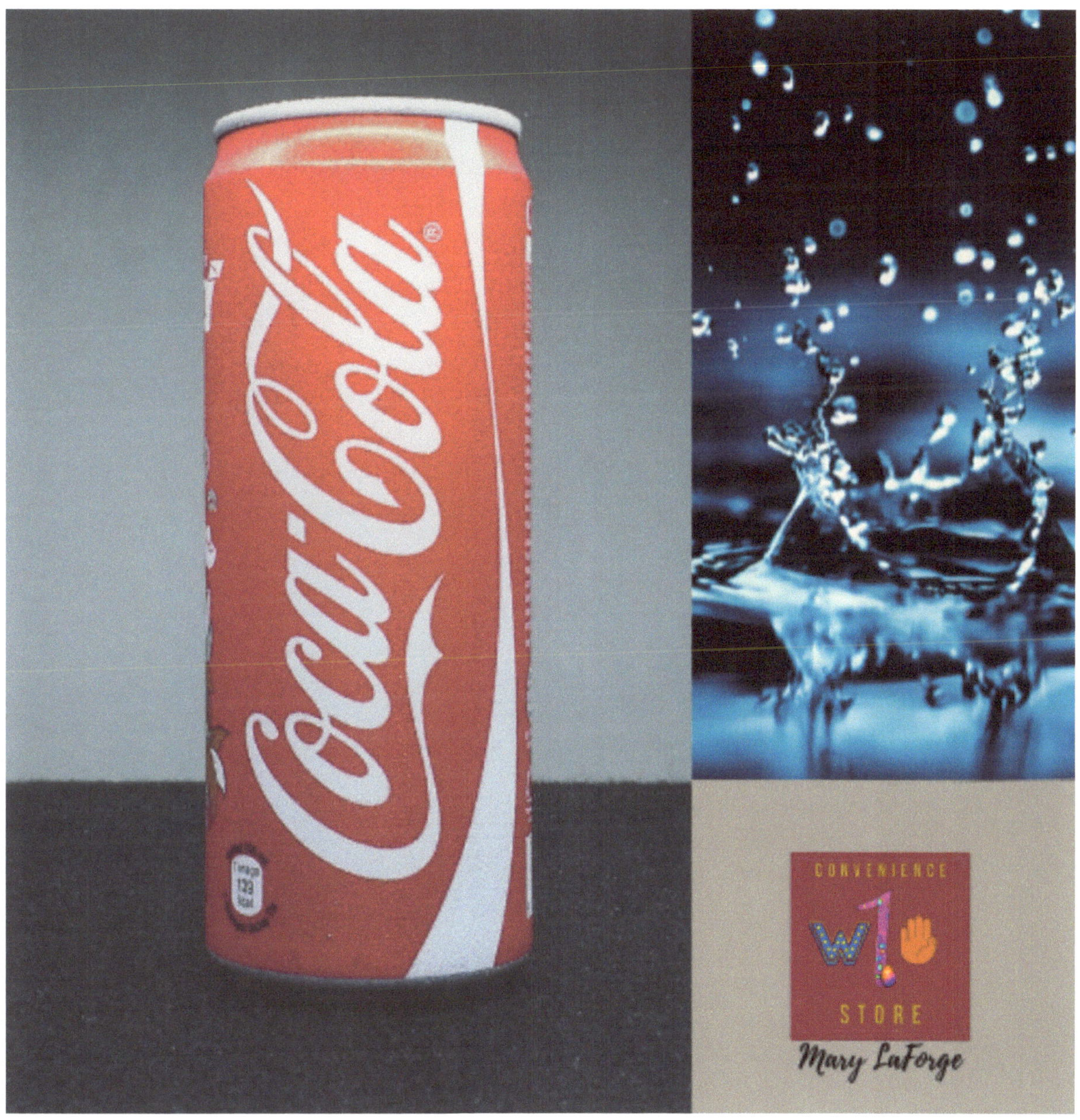

Coke and Water

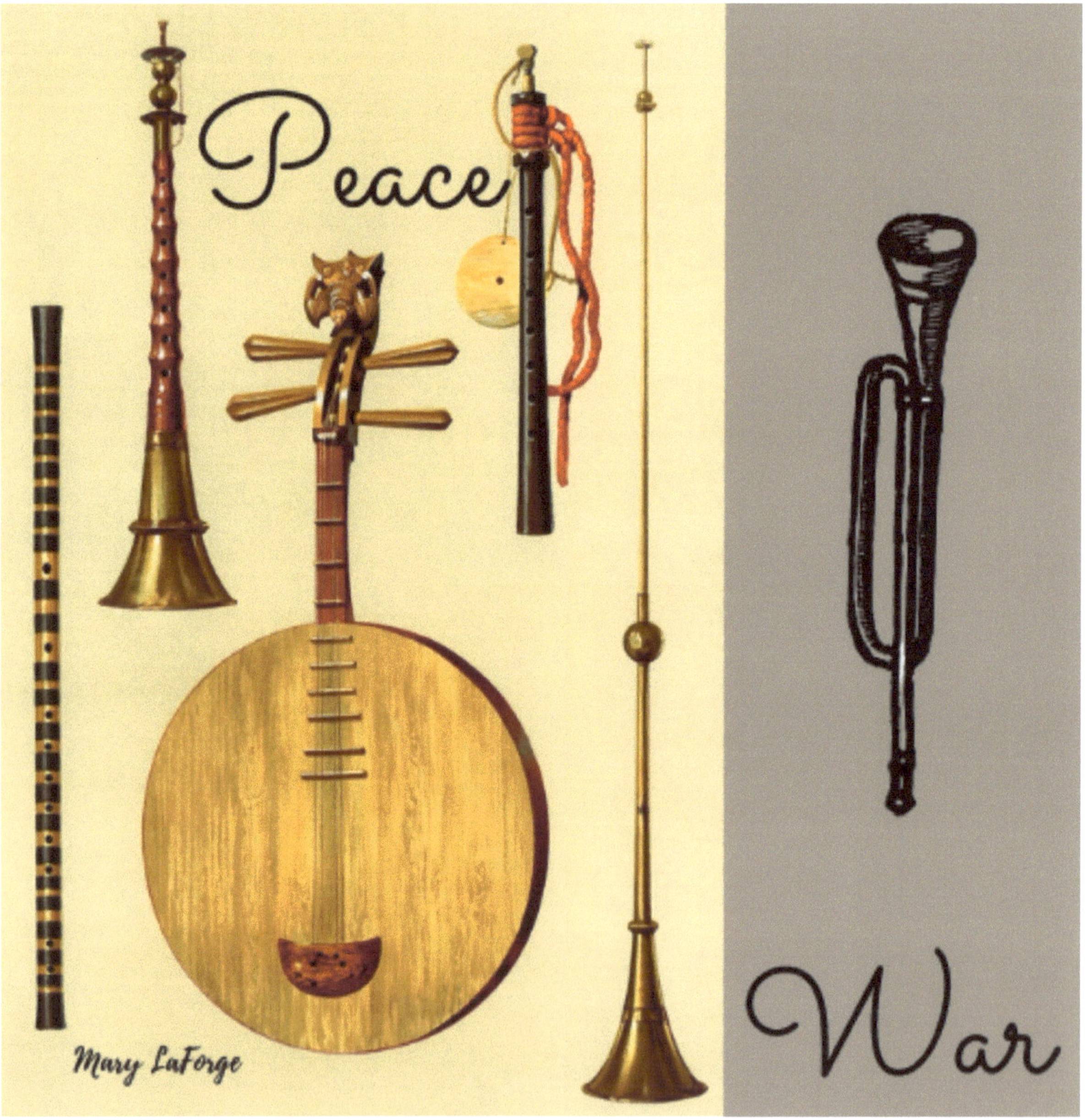

War and Peace

France.

Winning an Air France Art Award was a wonderful milestone in my art career. The award miraculously came with a one-week flight to Paris. I stayed in a 6th-floor 14th Arondissement walk-up rented by a German student and her Chinese boyfriend who was studying for his Ph.D. The room was clean and narrow with a large window view to the other rooftops. One morning my hostess woke me with two glasses and a bottle of red wine. She opened the window letting in the cold Winter air, sat at the small table and read poems by Rilke while I listened intently, warmed from the wine and the lovely down comforter.

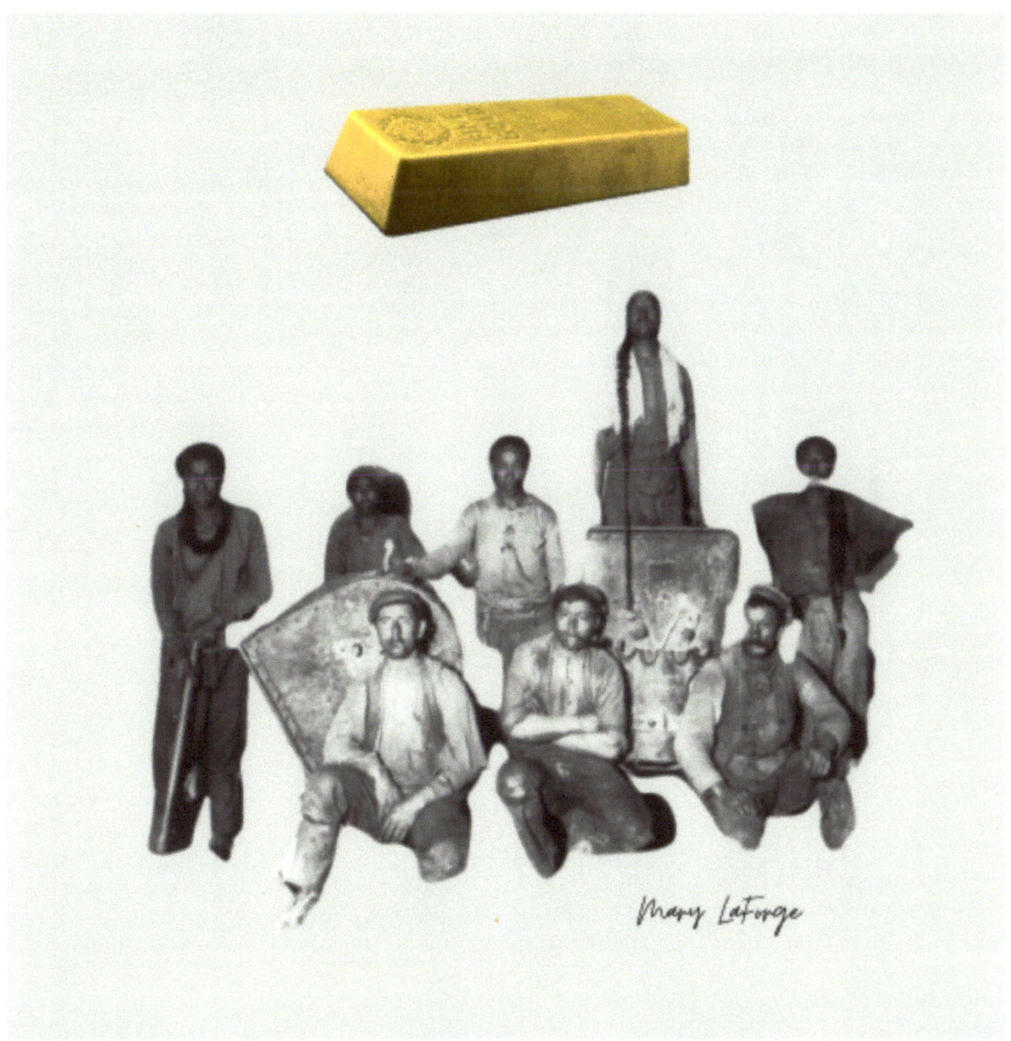

Gold Miners

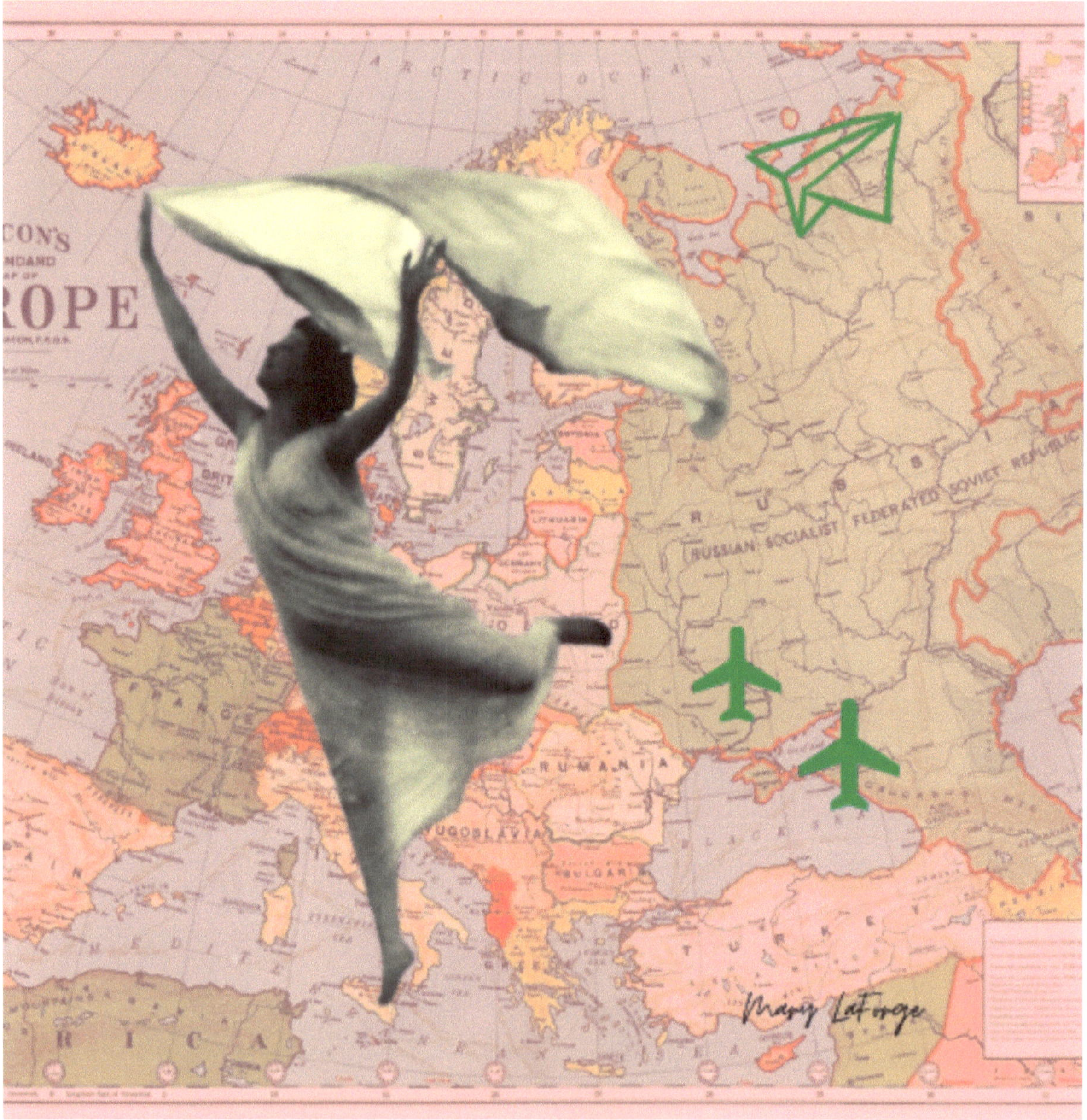

Femme Danseusse

French Print
ABCDEFGHIJKL
MNOPQRSTUVW
qrstuv
67890
Mary LaForge

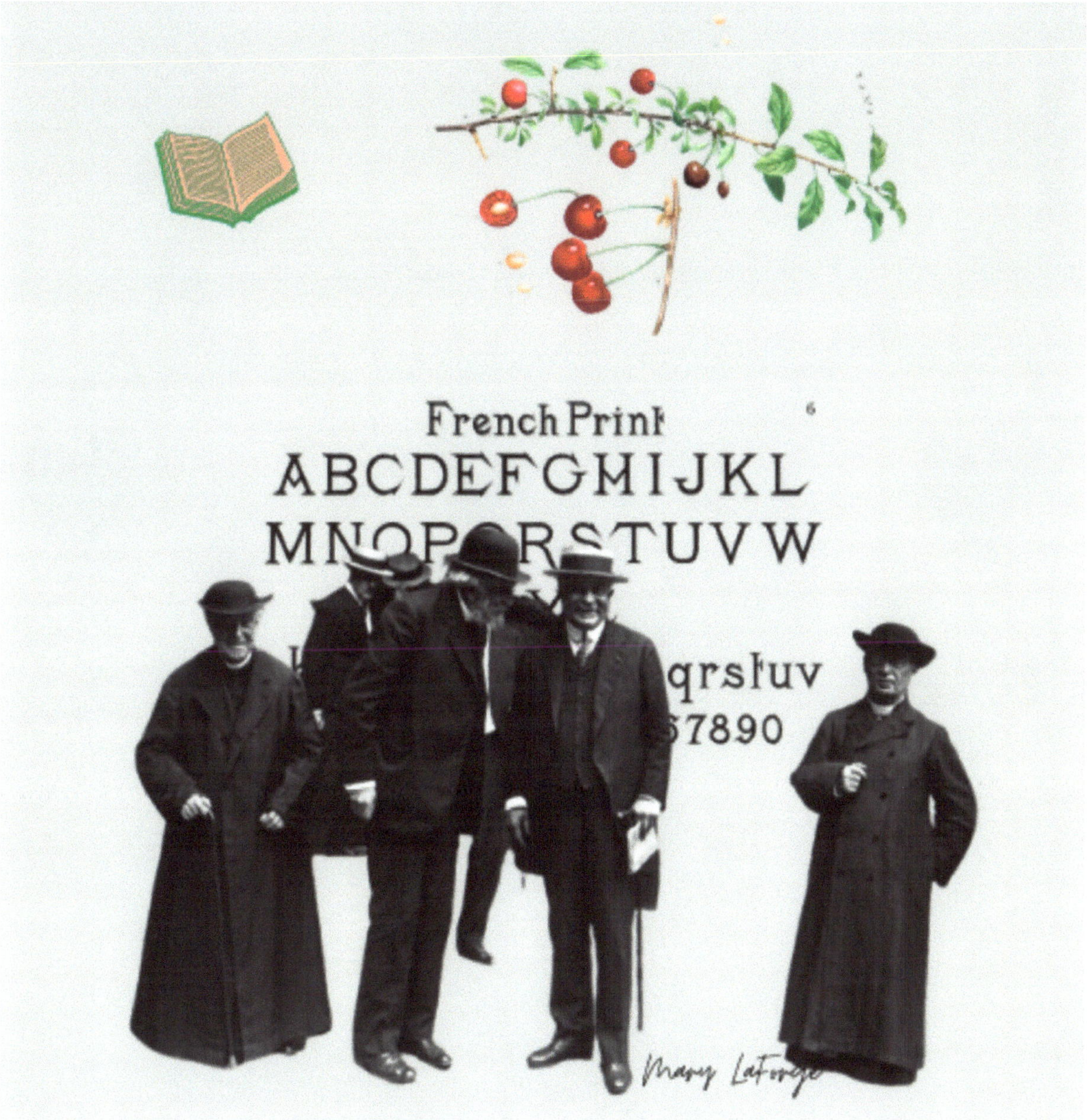

Words

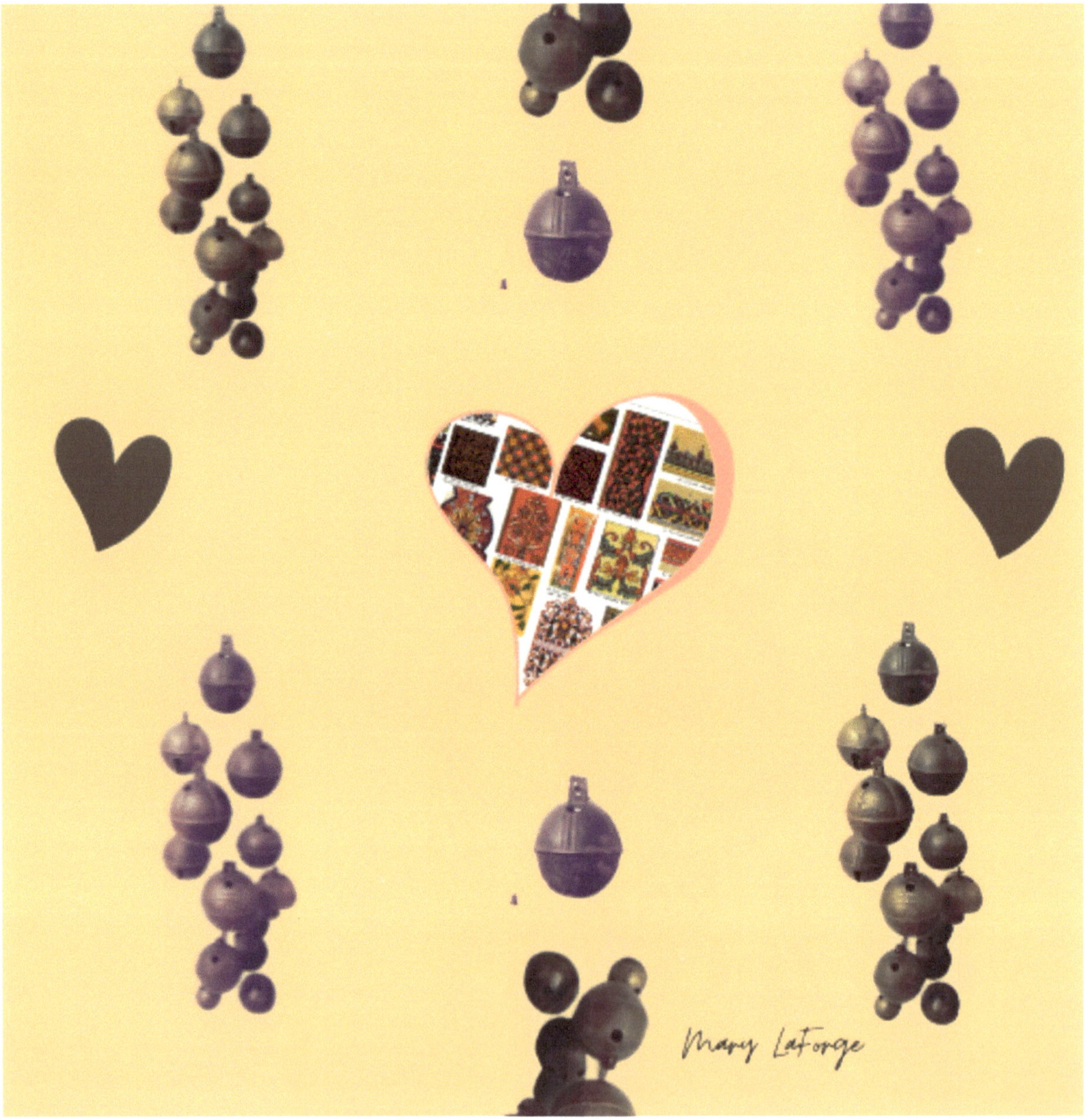

Wallpaper

China.

Fix your mind on truth, hold fast to virtue, rely on loving kindness, and find your recreation in the Arts -- **Confucius, The Analects**

Early 2018 I had a studio in Savannah, Georgia and spent most days painting with acrylics on canvas. With rent renewal coming up I made a decision to chuck making art for awhile and set out on an adventure. After downsizing and donating the body of work I had created there, I arrived in Nashville with little more than pen and paper and tablet. The next three months were spent writing poems about the AirBnB, places I ate, visited and wrote poems at, 30 in total.

My AirBnB Chinese hosts were lovely and went out of their way to make me feel comfortable. The Chinese New Year celebration with their Baptist church members was wonderful. One activity presented was a calligrapher, and I believe that was the beginning of my renewed interest in making art. When I moved further west Wri and Dan and 3-year-old Amber visited us and brought their homemade veggie dumplings that I loved so much. Dipped in vinegar and gobbled down with chopsticks, yum!

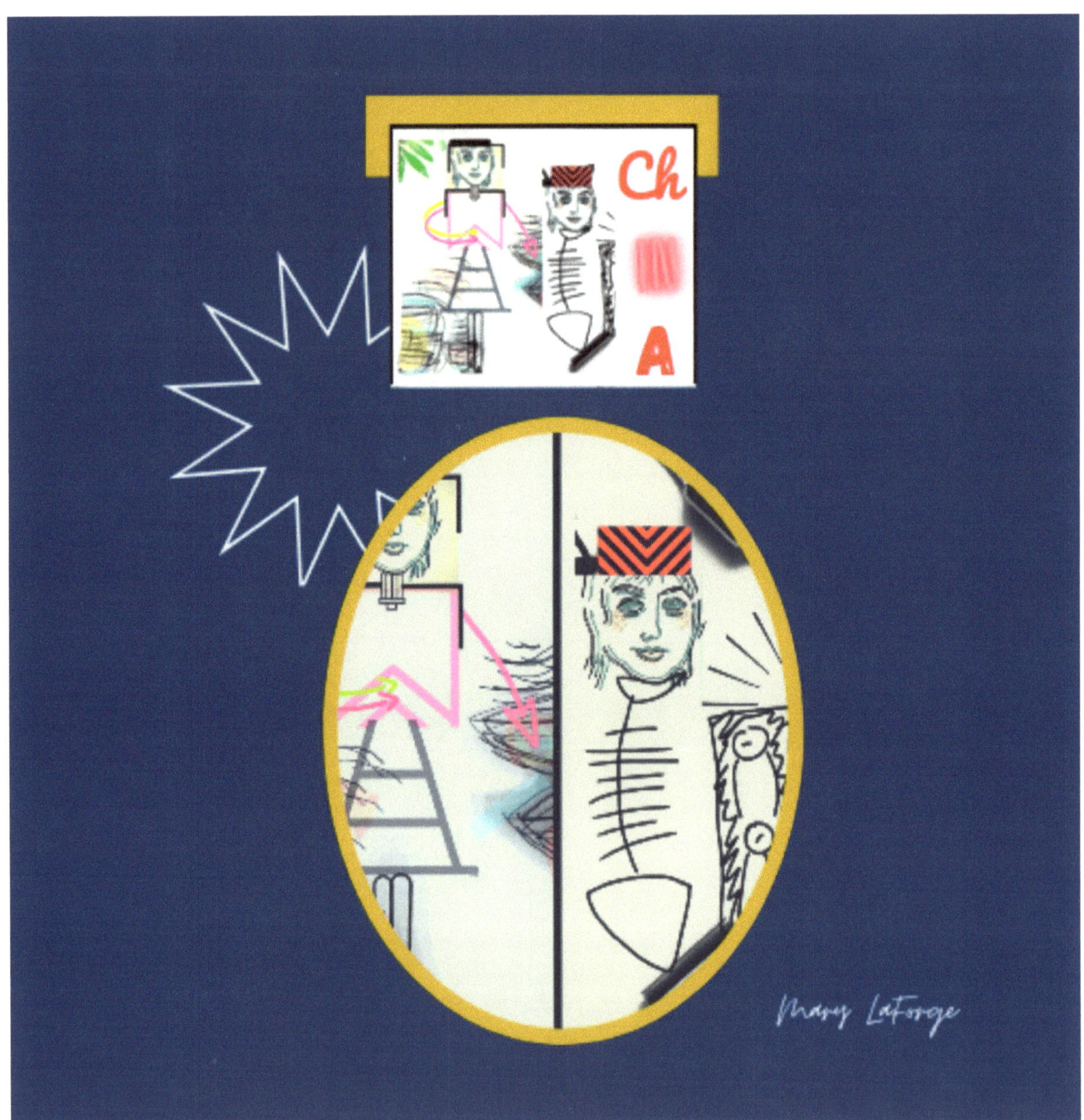

Not Ming Vase

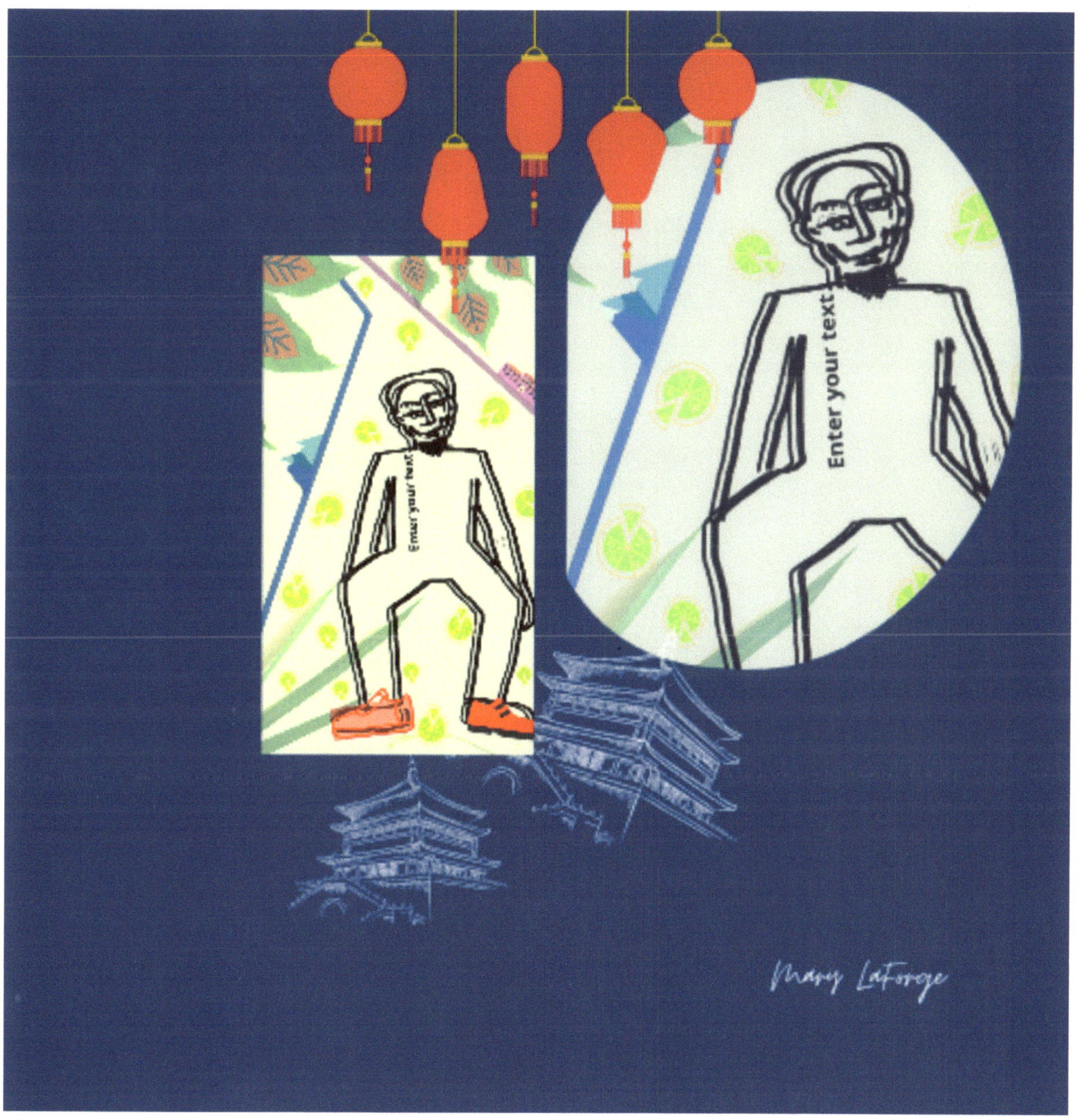

Hanging Lanterns

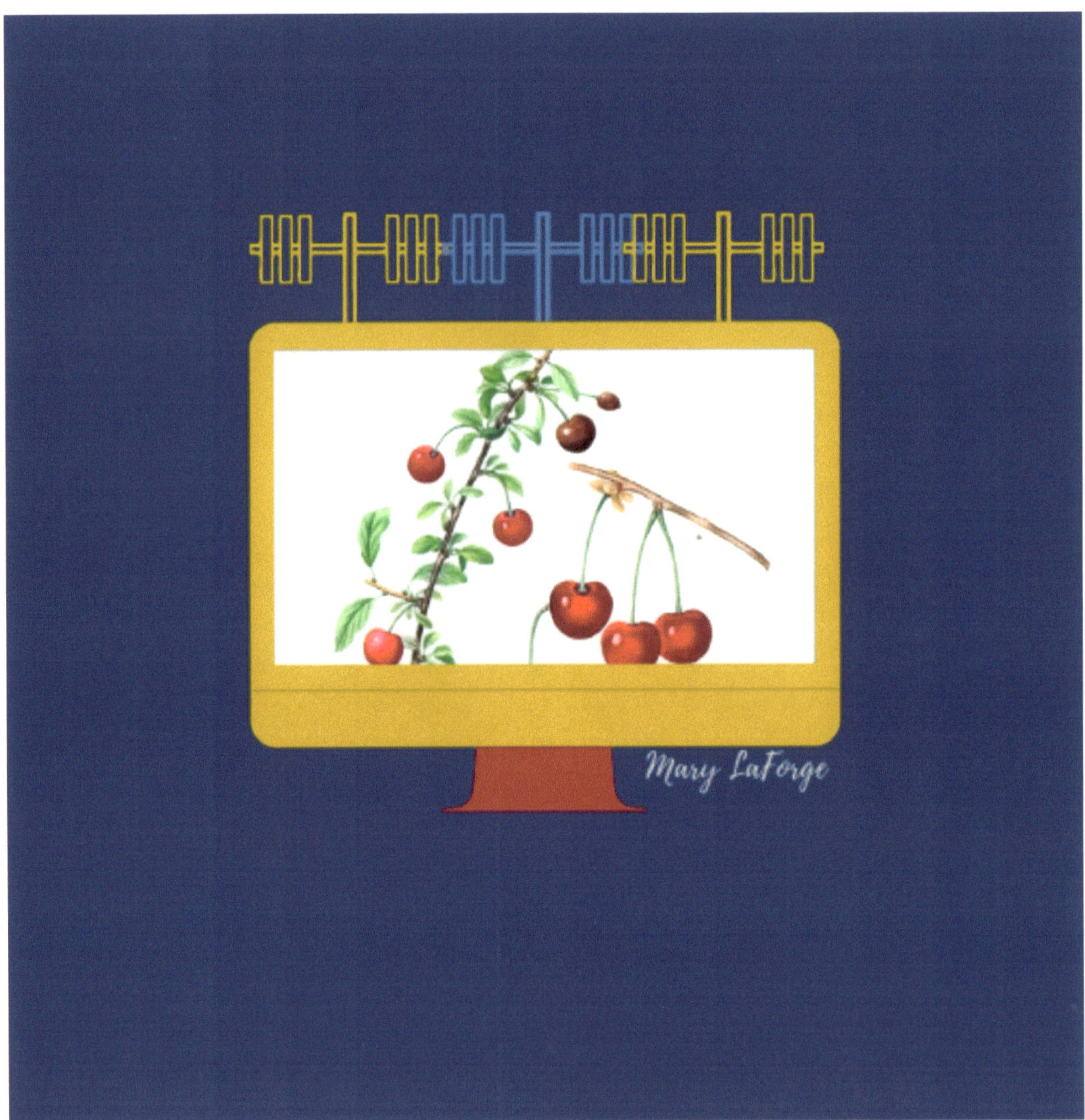

T - V Station

CHAPTER two

2022 calendar.

This chapter includes 12 digital artworks, one for each month of 2022, offered as limited editions. Stories about technique and personal references to the artist can be found on the artist's blog.

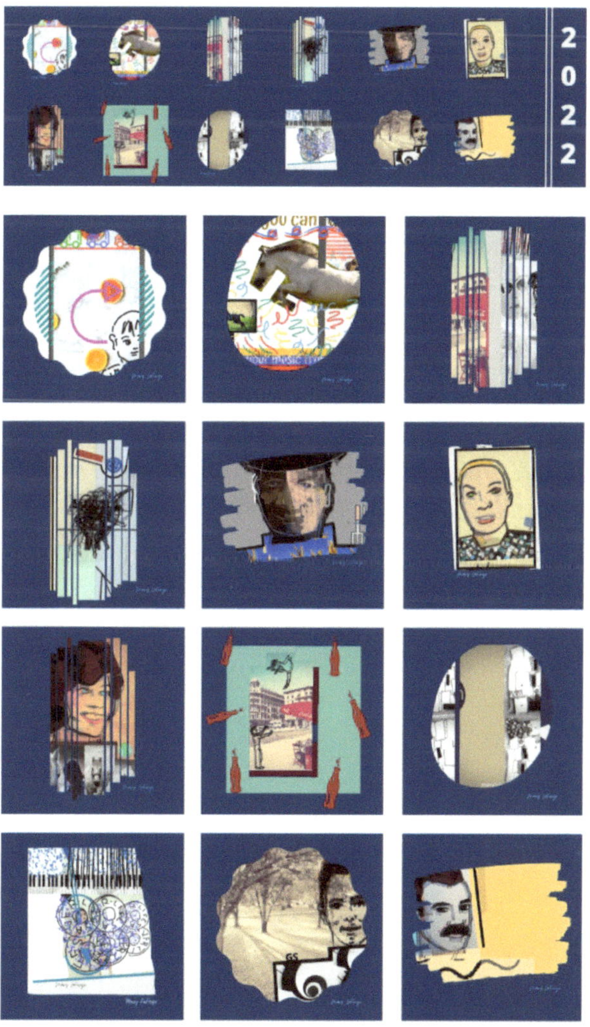

Mashup.

I've traveled elsewhere and interacted with many cultures. Artists in the past might have moved to different places during their lives and were influenced by their new surroundings, but for the most part their cultural influences were far less expansive than our outreach is today. Upward mobility aside, the Internet has brought culture to our home without necessarily having to visit places physically.

With the Internet came online platforms for creating art digitally. Artists could now reproduce their creations in multiples without the lithographic and other expensive printing methods for selling prints of their original artwork, through photography. Then digital creating software was introduced where artists could create a work of art directly from a computer screen. I jumped on that bandwagon.

One of the benefits of digital creating I particularly enjoy is the way innovation occurs. For instance, I could have a certain image or concept in mind and as I go about collecting and manipulating the disparate elements, I may make a mistake or place an asset in a space by accident and yet discover that the alternative is so much better than my original perception. It's a sort of going beyond into the unknown without fear because the remedy is a simple undo, and very satsfying. Working with oils you have to take drying time into consideration when making changes and that in between time is valuable for allowing the muse to process. Yet adjusting your digital organizational response time gets quicker, and digital painting becomes more like music where one note follows another, harmoniously, without stopping.

So, digital creating afforded me a way to collage by choosing from various time periods, textures, emotional content, etc. often overlapping these in hybrid fashion like an event taking place simultaneously at home and in a venue. That in itself is a mashup. My artistic voice has now become a mashup of elements in sync with a 21st Century post-pandemic world expressing a heritage evolving before our very eyes. And yet I bring the vintage past with me as metaphor of my personal and collective heritage.

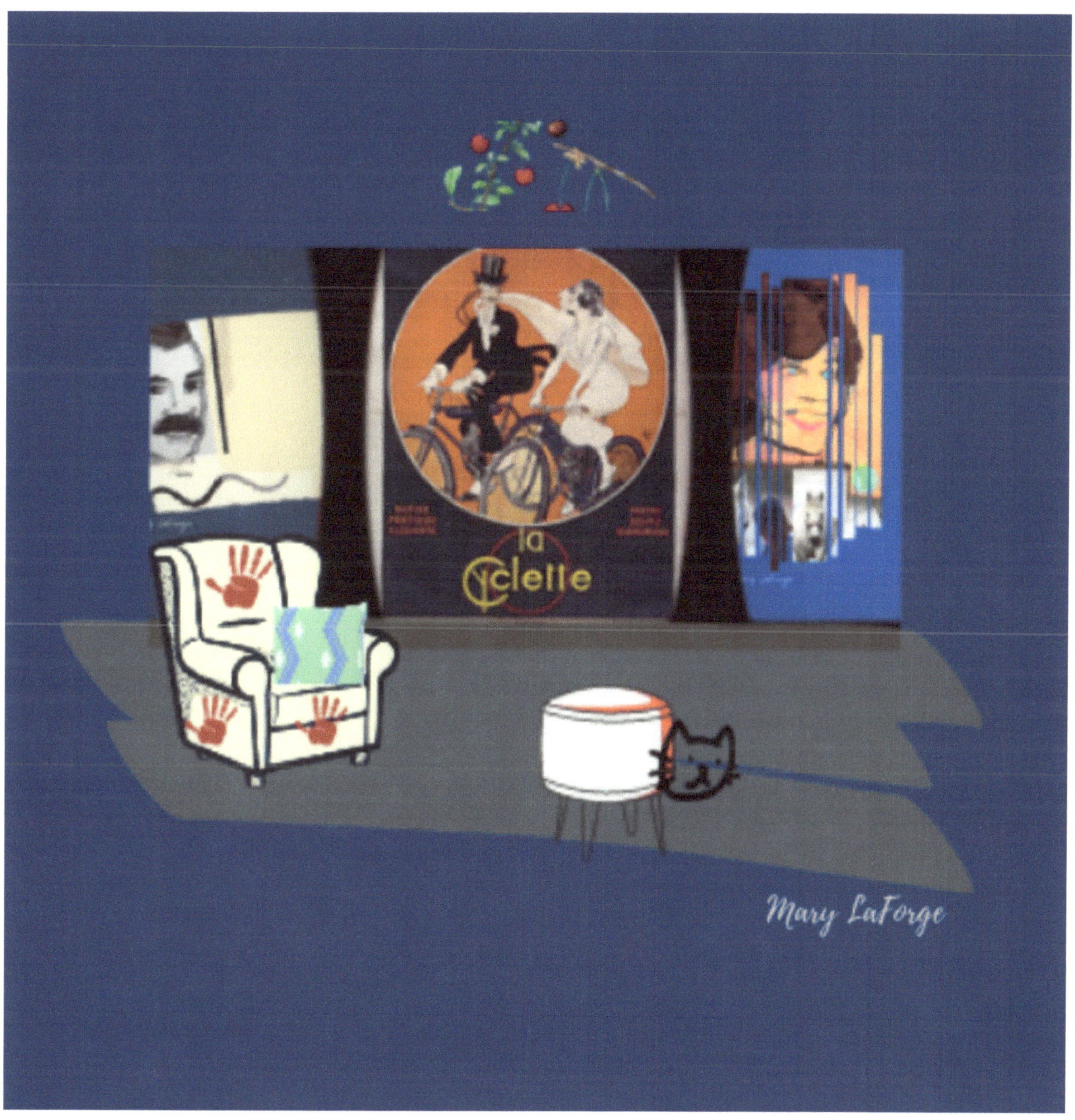

Kitty Kat Ottoman

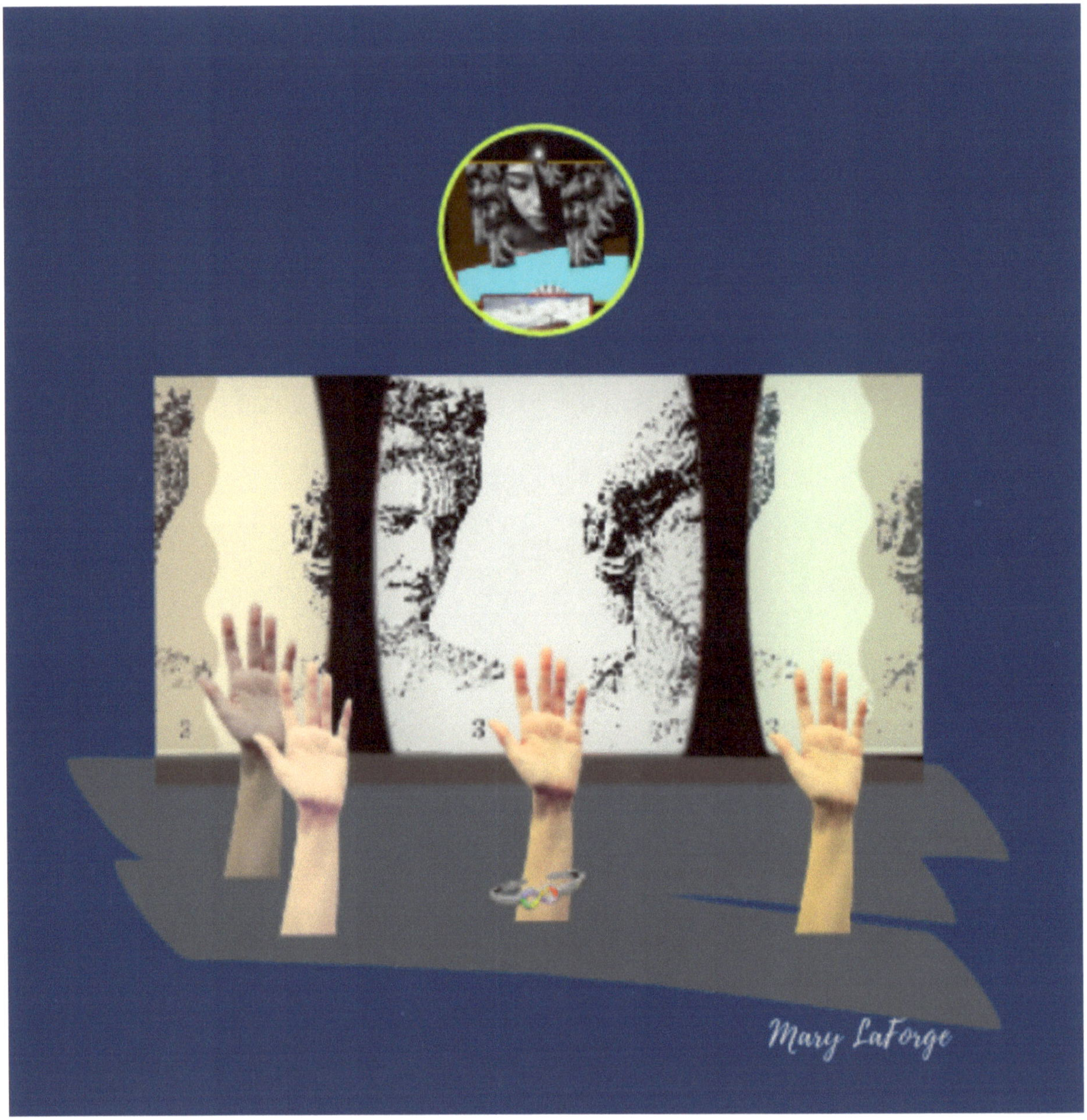

Hand Jive

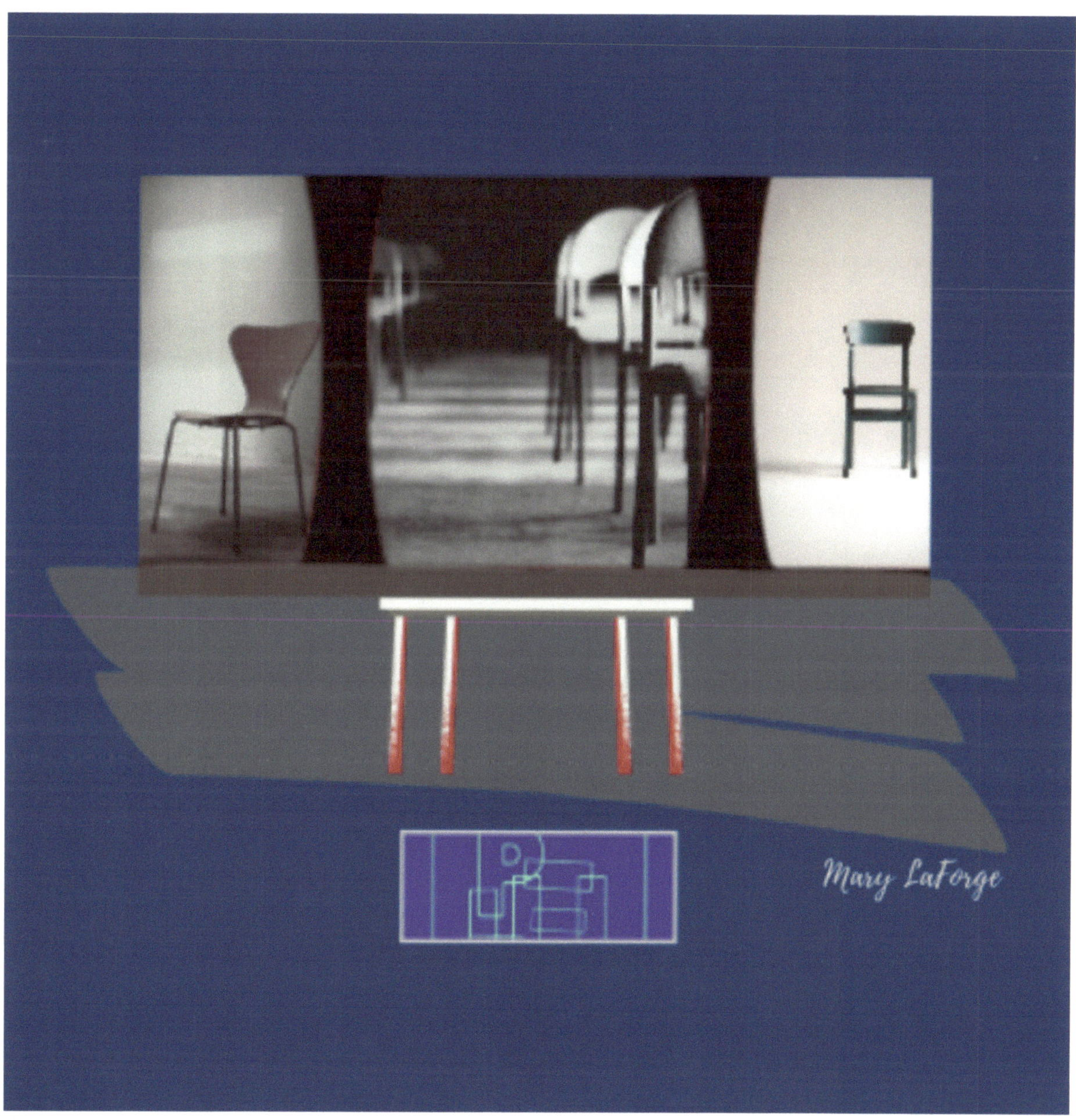

Table and Chairs I

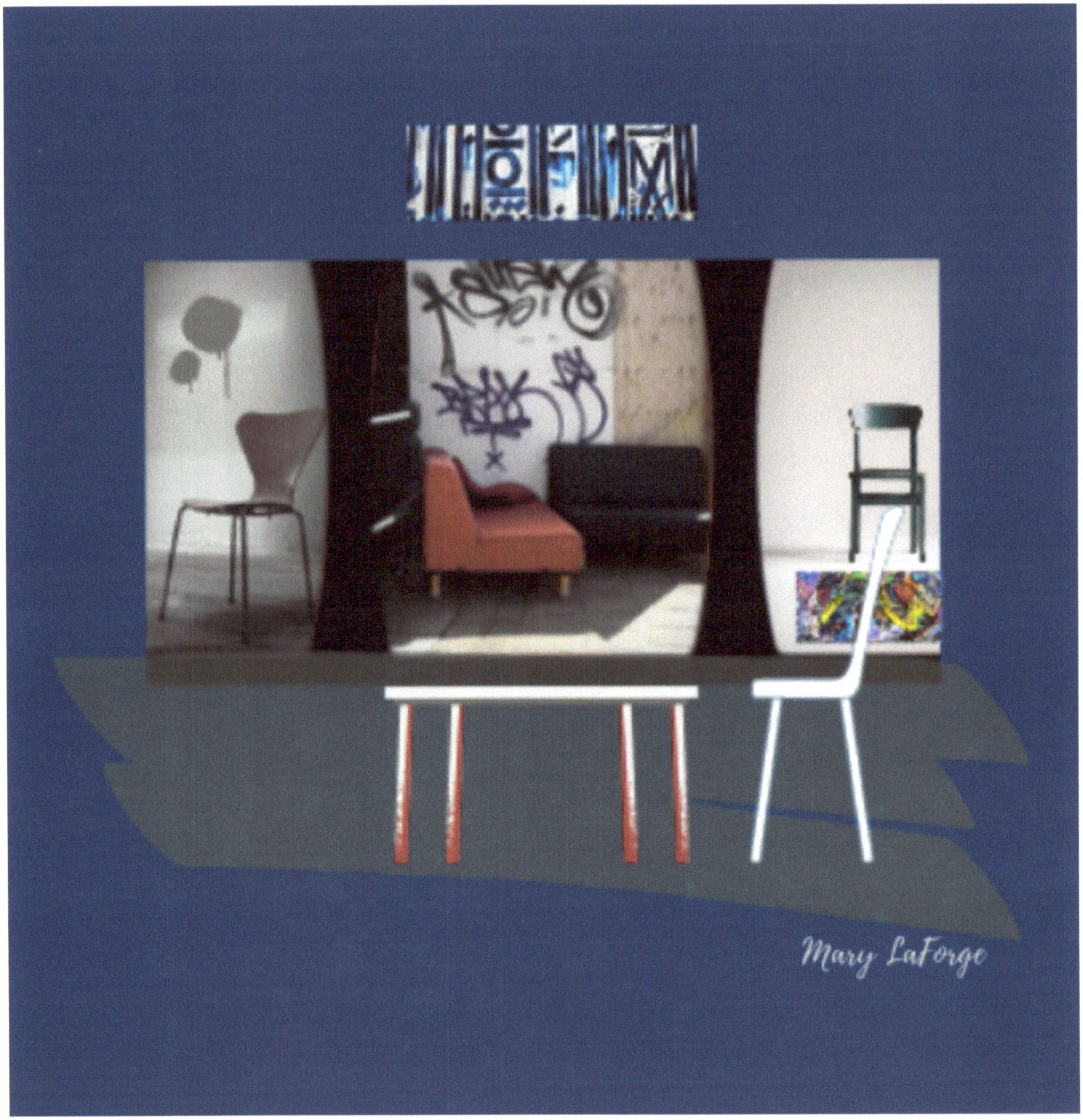

Table and Chairs II

The Future Of Art.

NFTs have adopted the art world. Basically though, nobody is buying NFT for the art. The art can't be displayed beyond the computer screen. An art wall of computer screens seems complicated and absent the sense of beauty an artwork usually activates in us. Instead, buying NFT art is primarily for monetary worth. An investment for investment's sake. Not art.

One artist currently using NFTs says his sketches and preliminary drawings are minted to use as digital presentations for his subsequent sculptures within proposals and client overview before he spends money on costly materials, as well as being his provenance tracker.

Sorting out the test phase of this and other technologies suitable for the art world may be a daunting task, yet one ultimately worth exploring.

CONCLUSION

Heritage vs. No Heritage.

Much of what motivates the involvement of the state and other organisations in heritage is related to the economic potential of heritage and its connections with tourism.

Archaeologist LaurajaneSmith, who has written extensively in the field of critical heritage studies, writes 'there is, really, no such thing as heritage' (2006, p,11).

-- two quotes from Open.edu https:// www.open.edu/ openlearn/history-the-arts/history/what-heritage/content-section-3

While we may think our heritage is being destroyed, those of us who lack a heritage notice that mostly illusions are what is really being destroyed.

Besides that, there's no such thing as time, as well as many other ideas we were taught to believe, because of our curiosity.

There's nothing to learn. There's nothing to teach. There's only collage. -- Alice Shapiro

ABOUT THE ARTIST

Alice Shapiro is winner of the Air France Art Award and the 2021 Literary Titan Silver Book Award. She also served four years as Poet Laureate, was nominated twice for a Pushcart Poetry Prize and is author of 5 published books. Shapiro currently lives in Tennessee.

www.ingramcontent.com/pod-product-compliance
Lightning Source LLC
LaVergne TN
LVHW071611180726
843512LV00003B/619